T. P. Wilson

Working in the Shade

Or Lowly Sowing Brings Glorious Reaping

T. P. Wilson

Working in the Shade

Or Lowly Sowing Brings Glorious Reaping

ISBN/EAN: 9783743398306

Manufactured in Europe, USA, Canada, Australia, Japa

Cover: Foto ©Lupo / pixelio.de

Manufactured and distributed by brebook publishing software (www.brebook.com)

T. P. Wilson

Working in the Shade

N THE SHADE;

OR,

LOWLY SOWING BRINGS GLORIOUS REAPING.

By

REV. T. P. WILSON, M.A.,
(*Vicar of Pazenham,*)
Author of "*True to his Colours, or, The Life that Wears Best,*'
'*Frank Oldfield, or, Lost and Found, &c.*

" How far that little candle throws its beams,
So shines a good deed in a naughty world
                                    SHAKESPEARE

THOMAS NELSON AND SONS,
LONDON, EDINBURGH AND NEW YORK

'The two walked slowly forward'
Page 17

THOMAS NELSON AND SONS,
LONDON, EDINBURGH, AND NEW YORK

Contents.

I	THE NEW COMER,	9
II	SETTLING DOWN,	21
III	"THE NEW SCHOOL,"	28
IV	WHAT IS UNSELFISHNESS?	37
V	THE STAMP OF THE CROSS,	53
VI	DUTY,	64
VII	THE SELFISH ISLANDS,	75
VIII	A LITTLE MYSTERIOUS,	102
IX	RUBY GRIGG,	114
X.	A ROUGH JEWEL POLISHED,	133
XI	A SURPRISE,	149
XII	CLOUD AND SUNSHINE,	167

'It's this here little Testament'

WORKING IN THE SHADE.

I.

The New-Comer.

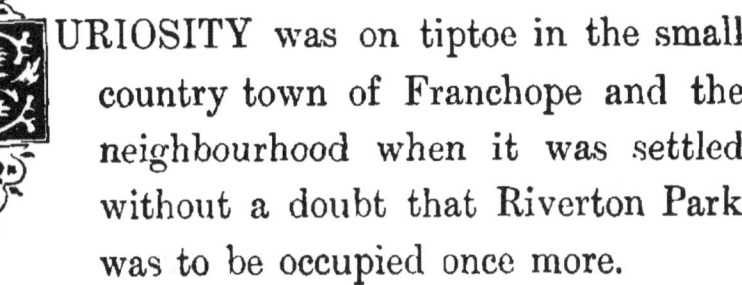CURIOSITY was on tiptoe in the small country town of Franchope and the neighbourhood when it was settled without a doubt that Riverton Park was to be occupied once more.

Park House, which was the name of the mansion belonging to the Riverton estate, was a fine, old, substantial structure, which stood upon a rising ground, and looked out upon a richly undulating country, a considerable portion of which belonged to the property.

The house was situated in the centre of an

extensive park, whose groups and avenues of venerable trees made it plain that persons of consideration had long been holders of the estate. But for the last twenty years Riverton Park had been a mystery and a desolation. No one had occupied the house during that time, except an old man and his wife, who pottered about the place, and just contrived to keep the buildings from tumbling into ruin. The shutters were always closed, as though the mansion were in a state of chronic mourning for a race of proprietors now become extinct, except that now and then, in summer time, a niggardly amount of fresh air and sunshine was allowed to find its way into the interior of the dwelling.

As for the grounds and the park, they were *overlooked* in more senses than one by a labourer and his sons, who lived in a hamlet called Bridgepath, which was situated on the estate, about a mile from the house, in the rear, and contained some five hundred people. John Willis and his sons were paid by somebody to look after the gardens and drives; and as they got their money regularly, and no one ever came to inspect their work, they just gave a turn at the old place now and then at odd times, and neither asked questions nor answered any, and allowed the grass and weeds to have their own way, till the whole domain became little better than an unsightly wilderness. Everybody said it was a shame, but as no one had a right to interfere, the broad, white front of Park House continued to look across the public road to Franchope through its surroundings of noble trees, with a sort of pensive dignity, its walls being more or less discoloured and scarred, while creepers straggled across the windows, looking like so many wrinkles indicative of decrepitude and decay.

But why did no one purchase it? Simply because its present owner, who was abroad somewhere, had no intention of selling it. At last, however, a change had come. Riverton Park was to be tenanted again. But by whom? Not by its former occupier; that was ascertained beyond doubt by those who had sufficient leisure and benevolence to find out other people's business for the gratification of the general public. It was not so clear who was to be the new-comer. Some said a retired tradesman; others, a foreign princess; others, the proprietor of a private lunatic asylum. These and other rumours were afloat, but none of them came to an anchor.

It was on a quiet summer's evening in July that Mary Stansfield was walking leisurely homeward along the highroad which passed through the Riverton estate and skirted the park. Miss Stansfield was the orphan child of an officer who had perished, with his wife and other children, in the Indian Mutiny. She had been left behind in England, in the family of a maiden aunt, her father's sister, who lived on her own property, which was situated between the Riverton estate and the town of Franchope. She had inherited from her father a small independence, and from both parents the priceless legacy of a truly Christian example, and the grace that rests on the child in answer to the prayers of faith and love.

The world considered her position a highly-

favoured one, for her aunt would no doubt
leave her her fortune and estate when she died;
for she had already as good as adopted her
niece, from whom she received all the attention
and watchful tenderness which she needed con-
tinually, by reason of age and manifold infirmities. But while our life has its outer convex
side, which magnifies its advantages before the
world, it has its inner concave side also, which
reduces the outer circumstances of prosperity
into littleness, when "the heart knoweth its
own bitterness, and a stranger doth not inter-
meddle with its joy." So it was with Mary
Stansfield. She had a refined and luxurious
home, and all her wants supplied. She was
practically mistress of the household, and had
many friends and acquaintances in the families
of the neighbouring gentry, several of whom
had country seats within easy walk or drive of
her home. Yet there was a heavy cross in her
lot, and its edges were very sharp. In her
aged aunt, with whom she lived, there were
a harshness of character, and an inability to
appreciate or sympathize with her niece, which

would have made Mary Stansfield's life a burden to her had it not been for her high sense of duty, her patient charity, and God's abiding grace in her heart. Misunderstood, thwarted at every turn, her attentions misinterpreted, her gentle forbearance made the object of keen and relentless sarcasm or lofty reproof, her supposed failings and shortcomings exposed and commented upon with ruthless bitterness, while yet the tongue which wounded never transgressed the bounds imposed by politeness, but rather chose the blandest terms wherewith to stab the deepest,—hers was indeed a life whose daily strain taxed the unostentatious grace of patience to the utmost, and made her heart often waver, while yet the settled will never lost its foothold.

How gladly, had she consulted self, would she have left her gilded prison and joined some congenial sister, as her own means would have permitted her to do, in work for God, where, after toiling abroad, she could come back to a humble home, in which her heart would be free, and generous love would answer love.

But duty said "No," as she believed. The cold, hard woman who so cruelly repulsed her was her beloved father's only sister, and she had resolved that while her aunt claimed or desired her services no personal considerations should withdraw her from that house of restraint and humiliation.

Pondering the difficulties of her trying position, yet in no murmuring spirit, Mary Stansfield, on this quiet summer's evening, was just passing the boundary wall which separated Riverton Park from the adjoining property, when, to her surprise and partly amusement also, she noticed a venerable-looking old gentleman seated school boy fashion on the top rail of a five barred gate. The contrast between his patriarchal appearance and his attitude and position made her find it difficult to keep her countenance; so, turning her head away lest he should see the smile on her face, she was quickening her pace, when she became aware that he had jumped down from his elevated seat and was advancing towards her.

"Miss Stansfield, I suppose?" he asked, as

she hesitated for a moment in her walk, at the same time raising his hat respectfully.

Surprised at this salutation, but pleased with the voice and manner of the stranger, she stopped, and replied to his question in the affirmative, and was moving on, when he added,—

"I am a stranger to you at present, my dear young lady; but I hope not to be so long. I daresay you will guess that I am the new occupier of Riverton Park. I suppose I ought properly to wait for a formal introduction before making your acquaintance; but I have lived abroad in the colonies for some years past, and colonial life makes one disposed at times to set aside or disregard some of those social barriers which are, I know, necessary in the old country; so you must excuse an old man for introducing himself, and will permit him, I am sure, to accompany you as far as your aunt's lodge.'

There was something so frank, and at the same time so thoroughly courteous, about the old gentleman's address that Miss Stansfield could not be offended with him; while his age and bearing prevented her feeling that there was any impropriety in her permitting him to be her companion on the public road till she should reach the drive-gate leading up to her home. She therefore bowed her assent, and the two walked slowly forward.

"You must know, Miss Stansfield," proceeded the stranger, "that I have both seen you before and have also heard a good deal about you, though we have never met till to day.—Ah, I know what you would say," he added, with a smile, as he noticed her look of extreme surprise and her blush of bewilderment. "You are thinking, What can I have heard about one who is leading such a commonplace, retired life as yours? I will tell you. I have been rather anxious to know what sort of neighbours I shall have round me here, so I have been getting a little reliable information on the subject wherefrom it matters not; and my informant has told me about an old lady whose estate adjoins Riverton Park, and who has a niece living with her who belongs to a class for which I have a special respect, and which

I may call 'workers in the shade.' Do you understand me?"

"Perfectly," replied his companion; "only I feel utterly unworthy of being included in such a class."

"Of course you do. And just for this reason, because you're in the habit of burning candles instead of letting off fireworks. and so you think your humble candles aren't of much service because they don't go off with a rush and a fizz. Is that it?"

"Perhaps it may be so," said the other, laughing.

"Well, do you remember what Shakespeare says?" asked the old man.

"'How far that little candle throws its beams,
So shines a good deed in a naughty world.'

Now, I want you kindly to answer me a question. It is this, Are there any unselfish people in Franchope or the neighbourhood?"

The question was put so abruptly, and was so odd in itself, that Mary Stansfield looked in her companion's face with a half misgiving. He noticed it instantly. "You're a little doubtful as to the old gentleman's sanity?" he said, laughing; "but I'm quite sane and quite in earnest; and I repeat my question."

"Really,' said the other, much amused, "it is a very difficult question to answer. I hope and believe that there are many unselfish persons in our neighbourhood, or it would be sad indeed."

"Ah! true," was his reply, "but hoping is one thing, and believing is another. Now, I've been half over the world, and have come back to my own country with the settled conviction that selfishness is the great crying sin of our day; and it seems to me to have increased tenfold in my own native land since I last left it. So I should very much like to meet with a specimen or two of genuine unselfish people; for I have some important work to do here, and I shall stand in need of truly unselfish helpers. Can you name me one or two?

"Well, sir, if you mean by unselfish persons those who really work for God's glory and not their own, I freely admit that they are, and I suppose always must be, comparatively rare."

"That is exactly what I *do* mean, my dear young lady; can you help me to find a few such unselfish workers in your own rank of life, and of your own sex?"

His companion was silent for a few moments, then she said slowly and timidly, "I judge, dear sir, from the tone of your questions that you are a follower of that Saviour who has set us the only perfect example of unselfishness."

"I trust so, my young friend," was the other's reply; "I wish at least to be so. Well, I see we have only a few more steps to bring us to your aunt's lodge. We shall meet again, I have no doubt, before long; and perhaps when we do I shall have more to say to you on the same subject. Farewell, and thank you." And with a courteous salutation he parted from her.

II.

Settling Down.

RESTORATION and improvement went on vigorously at Riverton Park. The front of the house soon lost its careworn appearance; the walks laid aside their weeds, and shone with a lively surface of fresh gravel; the shutters ceased to exclude the daylight; while painters and paperers, masons and carpenters, decorators and upholsterers soon brought the interior of the dwelling into a becoming state of beauty, order, and comfort.

And now the new proprietor was looked for with anxious expectation. His name had already got abroad, and all the gentry round were prepared to welcome Colonel Dawson when he should take possession of his newly acquired property. The colonel was an old retired officer, who had spent many years since leaving the army in one or more of the colonies. And now he was come home again, and intended to pass the rest of his days at Riverton. This was all that report could confidently affirm at present.

Was he an old bachelor or married? and if the latter, was his wife still living, and was there any family? Very conflicting rumours got abroad on this subject, but very little satisfaction came of them. All that could conclusively be gathered was that Park House was to have a lady inhabitant as well as the colonel; but that only a portion of the house was to be fully furnished. The appearance of a coachman daily exercising two noble carriage-horses was also hailed as a sign that the colonel did not mean to lead an unsociable life.

So Franchope and its neighbourhood were content, and watched the arrivals at the station day by day with patient interest. At length, in the first week in August, it was observed that the colonel's carriage drew up at the railway office to meet the evening train from London. From a first-class carriage there emerged three persons the colonel, an elderly lady, and a young man who might be some twenty years of age; a footman and a lady's-maid also made their appearance; and all drove off for Riverton Park. Who could count the pairs of eyes that looked out from various windows in Franchope as the carriage drove rapidly through the town? A glance, a flash and the new-comers were gone.

And now, in a few days, the whole household having twice occupied the family pews in the old parish church on the Lord's day, the neighbouring gentry began to make their calls.

The first to do so were Lady Willerly and her daughter. Her ladyship had discovered that she was distantly connected with the colonel, and hastened to show her interest in him as speedily as possible. Having cordially shaken hands with her and her daughter, Colonel Dawson turned to the lady and young man by his side and introduced them as, "My sister Miss Dawson; my nephew Mr. Horace Jackson." So the relationships were settled, and public curiosity set at rest.

Numerous other callers followed, and by all it was agreed that the family was a decided acquisition, a pity perhaps that there was not a Mrs. Dawson and a few more young people to fill the roomy old house and add liveliness to the various parties and social gatherings among the gentry. A younger man than the colonel would undoubtedly have been more to the general taste, especially as it was soon found that the family at Park House neither accepted nor gave dinner invitations, nor indeed invitations to any gatherings except quiet afternoon friendly meetings, where intercourse with a few neighbours could be enjoyed without mixing with the gaieties of the fashionable world.

So good society shrugged its shoulders, and raised its eyebrows, and regretted that the colonel, who doubtless was a good man, should have taken up such strict and strange notions. However, people must please themselves; and so it came to pass that the family at Riverton

Park was soon left pretty much to itself, just exchanging civil calls now and then with the principal neighbours, and being left out of the circle of fashionable intimacy

Three families, however, kept up a closer acquaintance, which ripened, more or less, into friendship. About a mile and a half from the Park, on the side that was farthest from Franchope, lived Mr. Arthur Wilder, a gentleman of independent means, with a wife, a grown up son, and three daughters. Horace Jackson was soon on the most intimate terms with young Wilder, and with his sisters, who had the reputation of being the most earnest workers in all good and benevolent schemes, so that in them the clergyman of their parish had the benefit of three additional right hands; while their parents and brother gave time, money, and influence to many a good cause and useful institution.

Adjoining the Riverton estate, in the direction of Franchope, was. as has been already stated, the property of the elderly Miss Stansfield, whose niece, Mary, has been introduced to our readers. The old lady was an early caller on the colonel's family, having made a special effort to rouse herself to pay the call, as she rarely left her own grounds. She at once took to Colonel Dawson; and, whether or no the liking was returned on his part, he frequently visited his infirm neighbour, and would spend many a quiet hour with her, to her great satisfaction. The old lady was one who wished to do good, and did it, but not graciously. So she had won respect and a good name among her dependants, but not love. The world called her selfish, but the world was wrong. She was self absorbed, but not selfish in the ordinary sense of the term. She acted upon principle of the highest kind; her religion was a reality, but she had been used ever to have her own way, and could not brook thwarting or contradiction; while her ailments and infirmities had clustered her thoughts too much round herself, and had generated a bitterness in her manner and speech, which made the lot of her niece, who was her constant companion, a very trying one.

To the north of Riverton Park was the estate of Lady Willerly. Her ladyship was one of those impetuous characters who are never content unless they are taking castles by storm; she must use a hatchet where a penknife would answer equally well or better. She was a widow, and dwelt with her only child Grace, a grown-up daughter, in her fine old family mansion, in the midst of her tenants and the poor, who lived in a state of chronic alarm lest she should be coming down upon them with some new and vigorous alteration or improvement. Her daughter was in some respects like her mother, as full of energy, but with a little more discretion bright as a sun beam, and honest as the day ; abounding also in good works. Such were the three families who maintained an intimacy with Colonel Dawson, when the rest of the neighbouring gentry dropped off into ordinary acquaintances.

III.

"The New School."

WHEN the family had occupied Park House about four months, a great deal of curiosity and excitement was felt by the inhabitants of Bridge path, the little hamlet of five hundred persons in the rear of Riverton Park, in consequence of sundry cart loads of bricks, stone, and lime being deposited on a field which was situated a few yards from the principal beer-shop. The colonel was going to build, it seemed, but what? Possibly a full grown public-house. Well, that would be a very questionable improvement. Was it to be a school, or a reading room?

There was a school already, held in the parlour of the blacksmith's cottage, where a master attended on week days, weather permitting, and imparted as much of the three R's as the children, whose parents thought it worth while to send them, could be induced to acquire under the pressure of a moderate amount of persuasion and an immoderate amount of castigation.

The master came in a pony-cart from Franchope, and returned in the same the moment the afternoon school broke up, so that his scholars had ample opportunity, when he was fairly gone, to settle any little disputes which might have arisen during school hours by vigorous fights on the open green, the combatants being usually encouraged to prolong their encounters to the utmost by the cheers of the men who gathered round them out of the neighbouring beer-shops.

As for religious instruction, the master, it is true, made his scholars read a portion of the Scriptures twice a week, and learn a few verses. But they would have been almost better without this; for the hard, matter of fact way in which he dealt with the Holy Book and its teachings would make the children rather hate than love their Bible lesson.

And what was done for the improvement, mental or spiritual, of the grown-up people? Nothing. Neither church nor chapel existed in the place. A few old and middle aged people walked occasionally to the nearest place of worship, some two miles off; but nine-tenths of the villagers went nowhere on a Sunday—that is to say, nowhere where they could hear anything to do them good, though they were ready enough to leave their homes on the Sabbath to congregate where they could drink and game together, and sing profane and immoral songs.

So Bridgepath was rightly called "a lost place:" and indeed it had been "lost" for so many years, that there seemed scarcely the remotest prospect of its being "found" by any one disposed to do it good. However, even in this dark spot there was a corner from which there shone a little flickering light. John Price and his family tenanted a tolerably roomy cottage at the entrance to the village, close to the horse pond. The poor man had seen better days, having acted as steward to the young squire from the time he came into the property till he disappeared with his infant son and an old nurse who had lived for nearly two generations on the Riverton estate. Poor John had served the squire's father also as steward, and loved the young master as if he had been his own child; and it was known that, when ruin fell on the young man, the poor steward was dragged down also to poverty, having been somehow or other involved in his employer's ruin. But never did John Price utter a word that would throw light on this subject to any one outside his own family. All he would let people know was, that the squire had left him his cottage rent-free for his life,—which was, indeed, all that the master had to leave his faithful servant.

The worthy man had struggled hard to keep himself and his family; but now he was bed-ridden, and had been so for some five or six years past. However, he had a patient wife, who made the most and best of a very little, and loving children, some of them in service, who helped him through. And he found a measure of peace in studying his old, well worn Bible, though he read it as yet but ignorantly. Still, what light he had he strove to impart to those of the villagers who came to sit and condole with him; while his wife, and an unmarried daughter who lived at home, both deploring the wickedness of Bridgepath, tried to throw in a word of scriptural truth now and then, for the sake of instructing and improving their heathenish neighbours.

It may be well imagined, then, with what interest all the villagers, but especially the Prices, including John himself, as he was propped up in bed and gazed through the casement, marked the numerous carts bringing building materials of all kinds to the village. All doubts on the subject, however, were soon brought to an end by a call from the colonel at John's house in the early part of November. After a few kind inquiries about his health and family, Colonel Dawson informed him that he was going to build at once a school and master's house in Bridgepath, with a reading-room attached to it, and to place there a married man of thorough Christian principles; one who would not only look after the ordinary teaching of the children, but would also, under the superintendence of the vicar, conduct a simple religious service on Sundays for the instruction of the villagers.

Bridgepath had from time immemorial been under the special supervision of the proprietors of Riverton Park, the whole hamlet being a portion of the property. The parish to which it belonged was extensive, and the parish church some five miles distant, Bridgepath being just on the borders of the next parish, in which parish the Park itself was situated. So, in former days, the chaplain at the house used to look after the people of the hamlet in a good-natured sort of way, by taking food and clothing to the sick and destitute, and saying a kind word, and giving a little wholesome advice, where he thought they were needed. But being himself unhappily possessed of but little light, he was unable to impart much to others, and the spiritual destitution of poor Bridgepath never seemed to occur to his mind at all. But now, for the last twenty years, neither squire nor chaplain had resided at Riverton; so that a very occasional visit from the vicar—who had more on his hands nearer home than he could well accomplish, and who, with others, was living in constant expectation of some one coming to the property and bringing about a change was all that had been done directly for the scriptural instruction and eternal welfare of the benighted inhabitants of Bridgepath.

Now, however, a mighty change was coming, and the dwellers in the hamlet were supposed to be highly delighted, as a matter of course, with the prospect. And, certainly, the hearts of old John Price and his wife and daughter did rejoice; but not so the hearts of most of the inhabitants, for they were thoroughly conscious that much of the goings on in their village would not bear looking into by those who feared God and respected human law. Bridgepath had been now for a good many years a *privileged* place in the eyes of poachers, gamblers, and Sabbath breakers, where the devil's active servants could hold their festivals, especially on the Lord's day, without fear of interruption from policeman or preacher. And the women were as bad as the men, they "loved darkness rather than light, because their deeds were evil." So the new school and reading room arose amidst the sneers and loudly-expressed disgust of the majority of the population; the proprietors of the beer shops being specially bitter in their denunciations of this uncalled for innovation on the good old times and habits, so long the favoured lot of a primitive and unsophisticated people, who had been quite content when left to their own devices, and could do perfectly well without these new-fashioned schemes, if only good people would just let them alone. The good people, however, saw the matter in a different light; and so, spite of all the grumbling and outspoken dissatisfaction, the buildings were completed in the spring, and the new schoolmaster and his wife took up their abode in Bridgepath.

Colonel Dawson had chosen his man carefully, and duly warned him that he would find his post at first no bed of roses. To which the master replied that he was not afraid of encountering his share of thorns; and that he doubted not but that with prayer, patience, and perseverance, there would be both flowers and fruit in Bridgepath in due time. As for opposition, he rather enjoyed a little of it, and trusted to be enabled to live it down. The colonel was satisfied, for he knew that he had chosen a man who had already proved himself to be no mere talker. So Bridgepath looked on in sulky wonder; but soon was constrained to acknowledge that, in their new schoolmaster, the right man had been put into the right place.

And now the colonel was very anxious to get the help of some earnest-hearted Christian lady, who would visit the sick and needy in the neglected hamlet, carrying with her Christ in her heart and on her lips; for his sister was too old to undertake such a work. His thoughts turned to Mary Stansfield. He would go and have a talk with the old lady her aunt about it.

IV.

What is Unselfishness?

COLONEL DAWSON took a deep interest both in Miss Stansfield and her niece. He understood them both, and pitied them both, but for very different reasons. He pitied the old lady because she was throwing away her own happiness and crippling her own usefulness. He pitied her because she was not what she might so easily have been; because she was storing up vinegar where she might have gathered honey: and was one of those of whom Dr. South says that "they tell the truth, but tell it with the tongue of a viper." He pitied Mary Stansfield, but with a pity mingled with profound respect and admiration. He pitied her that she should have to bear those daily raspings of the spirit which her aunt, half unconsciously, perpetually inflicted on her. And yet he could not altogether regret the discipline, when he marked how the trial was daily burnishing the fine gold of her character. Still, he pitied both, and was a frequent visitor at Morewood Court, partly because he marked how few were the friends who cared to stay at the house, and, more still, because he hoped to be of use in lightening the burden of both aunt and niece.

Colonel Dawson was one of those who love "working in the shade." Not that he was ashamed or afraid of working in the light, but he was content to pursue the less attractive and less ornamental paths of usefulness, which few comparatively cared to follow. And so he had set himself resolutely and prayerfully to the task of rearranging the character of one who, he was persuaded, was capable and desirous of doing good and great things, could she only be got to hold herself at arm's length from herself for a little while, and see herself in the glass of

God's Word, and as others saw her. He felt sure that there was good, practical sense enough in her mind, and grace enough in her heart, to make her yield to conviction when he should draw her on to see and acknowledge a better way; and then he knew that, when she should have been drawn out of the old self into a better self, she would duly appreciate and love her long suffering niece. But he was well aware that the old self would not surrender its throne without a severe struggle, and he was therefore not surprised to find the old lady's bitterness rather increase than diminish as through their conversations she was learning to become more and more dissatisfied with herself.

Her poor niece had to bear in consequence the burden of an increased irritability in her aunt's addresses to her. But she was greatly cheered when the colonel took an opportunity of seeing her alone, and assuring her that, spite of appearances to the contrary, the clouds were beginning to break, and that light and peace would shortly follow.

It was now the month of June; the school and reading-room at Bridgepath had got fairly established; the growlers and grumblers had nearly all of them subsided; and many long-benighted souls were receiving light with gladness.

"Pray excuse my calling so early," said the colonel, as he took his seat beside the elder Miss Stansfield, on a bright sunny morning. The drawing room window was open, and the ladies were seated on either side of it—the aunt half reclining on an easy-chair, the other occupying a low stool, with the open Bible from which she had been reading aloud on her lap.

Miss Stansfield received her visitor very cordially, but it was plain that the reading of the Holy Book had not imparted any sunshine to her spirit, and there were traces of recent tears in her niece's eyes.

The colonel saw this, but made no remark on it. For a few moments he gazed on the lovely garden, visible through the open window, without speaking; then he said abruptly, "I was thinking how selfish we naturally are; those beautiful flowers reminded me of it, and seemed to reproach me. God gives us such a profusion of colour, and harmonizes it so marvellously to delight us; and yet how ready we are to pick out, as it were, the sombrest tints in his dealings with us, and to keep our eyes fixed on them."

Miss Stansfield coloured slightly, and then said, after a pause, during which her niece did not look up, but nervously moved the leaves of her Bible, " Yes, I quite agree with you, Colonel Dawson; there is abundance of selfishness in our days, especially among young people. They seem to think of nothing but having their own way, and seldom condescend to admit that those who have been brought up in less en lightened days can have gained any wisdom by experience."

"Ah! I dare say," replied the other; " I've no doubt that young people, many of them at least, have a large share of this very unlovable quality. Perhaps we have all of us more of it than we should like to admit to ourselves. But now, to tell the truth, I am on the look out for one or two unselfish people; can either of you, my dear friends, help me to find them?"

"I think you will search in vain in *this* neighbourhood," said the old lady dryly.

"Nay, my dear Miss Stansfield, are you not a little uncharitable? Surely you can point me to some who love doing good, and forget themselves in doing it."

"I can say 'Yes' to the first but not to the last part of your question," was the reply. "There are plenty who love doing good, according to the popular estimate of goodness; but they love still more to be known and praised as the doers of it."

"Well," rejoined her visitor, "granting this in a measure, I should still like to know of some of these popular good doers. We must make considerable allowance for human frailty. Perhaps I shall be able to pick out a real jewel, where you have believed them to be only coloured glass and tinsel."

"I fear not, Colonel Dawson. However, I will mention a few of what I believe to be but counterfeit gems. There are the Wilders, for instance. Those girls are always doing good, and their brother too. You have only to look into the local papers to see what a broad stream of good works is perpetually flowing from that family. What with ecclesiastical decorations, Sunday school and day school *fêtes*, dancing at charity balls, managing coal and clothing clubs, and a hundred other things in which the world and the Church get their alternate share pretty evenly, that family is a perfect pattern of good deeds for everybody to look at, like the children's samplers, which their mothers point to with so much pride. as they hang up framed in their cottages."

The colonel looked grave, and said, " Then you do not consider that there are likely to be any unselfish workers in the Wilder family ? "

" You had better ask my niece, colonel. She will give you an unprejudiced opinion."

The other looked towards the younger lady, and said, " I am asking now in confidence, and with an object, not from mere idle curiosity, far less from any wish to pick holes in the characters and conduct of any of my neighbours. So, Miss Mary, kindly give me your opinion."

Thus appealed to, the younger lady replied, but evidently with much reluctance, "I fear that my aunt is right in her judgment of the Wilders. I dare not recommend them to you as likely to prove, in the truest sense, unselfish workers. They are very kind and good-natured, and no one can help liking them; but " and she hesitated.

"I understand you," said the colonel, "they would not come up to my standard, you think?"

"I fear not; but then I should be sorry to judge them harshly, only you asked my honest opinion."

"Oh, speak out, my dear, speak out," said her aunt; "they are but afflicted with the epidemic which has attacked all ranks in our day. Thus, where will you find a really unselfish servant nowadays? The old fashioned domestics who would live a generation in a family, mourn over an accidental breakage committed once in a quarter of a century, and count their employer's interest as their own, are creatures entirely of the past. And as with maid and man, so with mistress and master, old or young. 'What am I to get as an equivalent if I do this or that?' seems the prevailing thought now with workers of every kind."

"Ah yes," said the colonel thoughtfully, "there is too much truth in what you say; only, in the darkest night we may detect a few stars, and some very bright ones too, if we will only look for them. And I am looking for stars now, but I shall be quite content to get one or two of the second or third magnitude."

"I'm afraid you'll hardly be able to find any in this neighbourhood, for the clouds," said the old lady, with a smile, in which the bitter prevailed over the sweet.

"Nay, nay, my dear friend," cried the colonel cheerily, "don't let us talk about clouds this lovely June morning. I fear, however, that I must not look for what I want among the Wilders. I can readily understand that they might be unwilling to work in the shade, where there would be nothing to repay them except the smile of Him who will not let even the cup of cold water rightly given go unrewarded. What do you say to Lady Willerly's daughter? I have heard great things of her. They tell me she is one of the most unselfish creatures under the sun."

"Ay," said the old lady dryly, "when the sun shines on her; but you want workers in the shade. Grace Willerly will not do for that."

"You think not? Well, let me tell you what I have heard of her. Those who know her well say that she never seems so happy as when she is doing good and making others happy. Her mother calls her 'my sunbeam.' She seems to take a pleasure in thwarting herself in order to gratify others. If she wants to go out for a walk, and some tiresome visitor comes in, she will laugh, and say, 'I was just wanting some one to come and keep me in, for I dare say I should have caught cold if I had gone out just now.' Or it may be quite the other way. She is just sitting down to draw or play, and some one calls and asks her to take a walk, and she at once leaves her occupation, jumps up, and says, 'Ah, how nice this is! I ought to take exercise, but felt disinclined; and you've come at the very right time, to entice me out.' In fact, her greatest pleasure seems to be to cross her own will and inclinations, that she may do what will give pleasure to others. Such is the picture that intimate friends have drawn of her; and certainly it is a very charming one. What say you to it, Miss Mary?"

"It is very beautiful, Colonel Dawson—" and she hesitated.

"Ah, then, too highly coloured, I suppose you would say. Give me your candid opinion."

"It is very difficult to say what I feel," replied Mary Stansfield, "without seeming to lay myself open to the charge of censoriousness or captiousness; and yet I cannot help seeing a shade of unreality, and even insincerity, on that bright and beautiful character, that it wants, in fact, one essential element of genuine unselfishness."

"Of course it does," broke in the elder lady; "you mean that it is not free from self-consciousness and, more or less, of parade."

"I fear so, dear aunt. I cannot help thinking that, as some one has said of faith, so it may be said of true unselfishness, that 'it is colourless like water,' it makes no show nor assertion of itself. But dear Grace Willerly is a sterling character for all that."

"So then," said the colonel, after a pause, "I must give up in despair, must I? No, that will never do Now, I am wanting a quiet worker in the shade for poor Bridgepath,— some young lady friend who has a little leisure time, and will go now and then and read in the cottages there the Word of God, and give some loving counsel to those who need it so much. I have the good vicar's full consent and approbation, he will gladly welcome any such helper as I may find for the post. It will be a true labour of love; and, without any more words I am come to ask Miss Stansfield if she will spare her niece for the good work, and Miss Mary if she will be willing to undertake it."

The reply of the two ladies, who were equally taken by surprise, was in each case made in a single word, and that word very characteristic. "Impossible!" cried the old lady. "Me!" exclaimed the younger one.

"Nay, not impossible, dear friend," said the colonel gently. "I want this service of love only once a week for an hour or two, and I am sure you can spare my young friend for that time. And as for yourself, Miss Mary, I believe, from what I have seen of you, that you are just fitted for the work; and I am sure that you are too sincere to excuse yourself on the ground of an unfitness which you do not really feel."

"And what am I to do?" asked the old lady bitterly.

"Exercise a little of this true unselfishness, dear friend. You see there are many ways in which you too can show true unselfishness in the cause of that Master whom I know you truly love, though he has laid you aside from much active work for him."

Miss Stansfield did not answer for a time;

she looked pained, but the bitterness had passed away from her countenance. Evading an immediate reply, she said, "I don't understand these many ways in which I can show unselfishness, Colonel Dawson."

"Do you not? May I mention some?"

"Yes, do," she replied earnestly.

"Well, bear with me then, while I make one or two suggestions which our late conversations have been leading up to. I will imagine myself in your place, and looking out to see where I may best put the stamp of the Cross on my life. I am wishing to do good, I am trying to do good; but may it not be that my benevolence is sometimes rendered so ungraciously that it gives more pain than pleasure to those who receive it? Ah, then, I will put the stamp of the Cross here. I will try, not only to do good, but to do it graciously. Perhaps, again, I am looking upon suffering and natural infirmity of temper as an excuse for harshness and hard judgment, and not as a call to exercise charity, patience, and forbearance. Then let me put the stamp of the Cross here also. Or, once more, perhaps I am in the habit of looking for the weeds rather than the flowers, for the shadows rather than the sunshine, in my lot. Well, then, here again I may place the stamp of the Cross, by exercising quiet, unostentatious self denial and unselfishness before the loving eyes of him who has made us for himself, and redeemed us that we might in all things glorify him. Might I not thus, dear friend, exhibit true unselfishness, and at the same time brighten my own heart, and also the hearts of others?"

No one spoke for a few moments, but the old lady bowed her head upon her hands and wept silently. Then she stretched out a hand to the colonel, without raising her head, and said in a half-stifled whisper, "Thank you, thank you, faithful friend. Mary shall under take the post if she will."

Ah yes! light had shone into that clouded spirit; the shadows were passing away. Mary Stansfield knelt her down by the old lady's side, and in one loving, tearful embrace, such as they had never known before, the icy barrier that had so long chilled that young and loving heart was melted, and there was peace.

The colonel was more than satisfied. He knew, as he quietly stole out of the room without a further word, that he had been privileged to gain that morning two like-minded workers in the shade, instead of one.

V.

The Stamp of the Cross.

A FEW days after Colonel Dawson's happy interview with Miss Stansfield and her niece, a *fête* was given by the Wilders at their residence, Holly House, partly for the entertainment of the children who belonged to the Sunday-school classes taught by the Misses Wilder, and partly also as a means of gathering together as many neighbouring friends and acquaintances as might be at leisure to come.

Colonel Dawson and his nephew had received a pressing invitation; and also Lady Willerly and her daughter, though the latter was hardly expected, as it was known how many engagements she had to tie her at home. The invitation, however, decided Grace Willerly to write at once and say that, although she had a very pressing engagement, she would arrange to put it off, as she felt that a good game of play with the dear children on the lawn at Holly House would be just the very thing she wanted to do her good and freshen her up.

So a large party assembled on the day appointed, and among them the colonel and his nephew the former because he wished to keep on friendly terms with his neighbours, though he anticipated but little pleasure from this particular gathering. Besides this, he was a little anxious to see to what extent the intimacy between the young Wilders and his nephew had gone; for he had something of a misgiving that the young man might be getting entangled in the attractions of one of the young ladies, and this was the last thing he would have desired for him. As for Horace Jackson himself, his impression concerning the younger members of the Wilder family was that they were decidedly "jolly." He had not yet consciously arrived at a warmer stage of feeling in regard to any one of them, and his estimate was tolerably correct. Somebody had characterized the young ladies of Holly House as "dashing girls," and such they certainly were.

The eldest was now about one and twenty, a fine *manly* young woman, with a loud voice, and very demonstrative manners, who seemed inclined to do good in the spirit of a prize-fighter, by attacking the evils which she sought to remedy with a masculine vigour, such as would drive them in terror off the field. The second daughter, Clara, was of a rather less commanding appearance than her elder sister, but dressed and talked pretty much in the same fashion. The third, Millicent, would naturally have been quiet and retiring, but had constrained herself to imitate her sisters. She had, however, only so far succeeded as to acquire an abrupt and off-hand style of speaking, which was calculated to shut up old-fashioned people, who had been brought up under the impression that young ladies should belong to the feminine gender. Indeed, when the three Misses Wilder were met on the public road in their walking attire, with natty little hats on their heads, ulsters down to their feet, turn-down collars round their necks, and riding-whips or walking-sticks in their hands, it would have been very difficult for an unpractised observer to determine to what particular sex they belonged.

Their brother was proud of his sisters, and matched them admirably. He was a kind-hearted, outspoken, generous young man, up to anything, from a midnight spree to a special religious service; hating everything like cant as decidedly "low," and going in for sincerity, truth, and free thought. Moreover, he spent his money, or, more strictly speaking, his father's money as well as his own, on horses, dogs, and guns, and left sundry little bills to stand over till the poor creditors had lost both hope and patience.

It was now four o'clock, and the children were assembling for tea, after a series of games, in which they had been joined by Grace Willerly with an unflagging energy, and been occasionally encouraged by a kind word from Mr. and Mrs. Wilder and their daughters.

"What a charming sight, isn't it?" said Mrs. Wilder to Colonel Dawson, as they strolled up to the tea-tables, which had been set out under the shade of some huge elms. "How happy the dear children seem!"

"Yes," replied her guest; "it is indeed a pleasant sight, and I am sure we may well learn a lesson of contentment with simple pleasures from the hearty enjoyment of these young ones. What a pity that the world and its attractions should ever get a place in the hearts of these or of any of us, since God has made us for purer and higher things!"

"Ah! very true, colonel,—but won't you come into the house? I see our friends are gathering in the drawing room. We shall find tea there; and Clara and Millicent, with Grace Willerly, will see that their little friends want for nothing. Oh! here is your nephew. Pray, Mr. Jackson, come in with us; I am sure you will be glad of a little refreshment."

So the elder guests assembled in the drawing-room, and got through an hour of miscellaneous gossip very creditably; at the end of which all adjourned to the garden again, and strolled about in twos and threes till the school children were dismissed and it was time for the visitors to take their leave.

"What a relief!" exclaimed the colonel to his nephew, as they trotted on side by side on their ride homewards.

"Well, it was dull work, uncle, I allow," said the young man, laughing. "But these gatherings are, I suppose, useful and necessary, if people are to keep up friendly acquaintance with one another, and do what is civil and neighbourly."

"Yes, perhaps so," replied his uncle; "but such an afternoon is little better than bondage and lost time at any rate to a man of my colonial habits. However, it has given me an opportunity of seeing more of the young ladies at Holly House."

"And I am afraid, uncle, that you do not find them improve upon acquaintance."

"Just so, Horace, they don't suit my taste at all."

"And yet, dear uncle, with all their dash, and *brusquerie*, and fastness, they really are most kind-hearted and unselfish girls."

"Kind-hearted, I allow, but I doubt their unselfishness."

"But why, uncle? what would you have more? They certainly don't spare themselves. They are here, there, and everywhere, when any good is to be done, and think nothing of spending any amount of time and money in making other people happy"

"True, Horace, but there is a pleasurable excitement in all this which more than overbalances any trouble it may cost, especially when the world's applause for their good deeds is thrown into the same scale"

"But," remonstrated the young man, in rather a disturbed and anxious tone, is not this dealing them a little hard measure? Where shall we find anything that will deserve the name of unselfishness, if we weigh people's actions too rigorously?"

"Ah! you think me severe and uncharitable, Horace. But now, it just comes to this. What do the Misses Wilder and their brother (for I suppose we must take him into consideration too) really forsake or give up in order to do good? I don't pretend to know the private affairs of the family generally, but certainly there are strong rumours afloat that the maxim, 'Be just before you are generous,' is not acted upon by the young people in their money concerns. I allowed just now that they are good-natured, but good nature is a very different thing from unselfishness. What personal gratification do they surrender in order to do good? What worldly pleasure or amusement do they deny themselves? What extravagance do they curtail?"

"I can't say much for them in that respect, certainly," replied the young man thoughtfully; "indeed, I must frankly confess that I have heard more than once from the eldest Miss Wilder the expression of her hope and conviction that the united good deeds of the family would be accepted, by the world at any rate, as a sort of atonement for follies and excesses which clearly could not be justified in themselves."

"I can well believe it, my dear nephew: but I have something much weightier to say on the subject, and it is this. There is manifestly one great want in all the doings of these kindhearted people at Holly House, which would make me at once deny the character of unselfishness to their best deeds."

"And what is that, dear uncle?"

"The stamp of the Cross, Horace. I know that there are plenty of crosses about them,— crosses on their prayer books, crosses round their necks, crosses on their writing cases and on their furniture; but *the* Cross is wanting. In a word, they are not denying self, and seeking to do good to others from love to that Saviour who gave up so much for them. I know that they are not without religion in the eyes of the world; but I cannot, I dare not believe that they are really actuated by love to the great Master in what they may do to make others happy. Am I wrong, Horace?"

"No, uncle, I cannot say that you are. Much as I like the girls on many accounts, I should not be speaking my honest sentiments were I to say that I believed them to be doing good to others from real Christian motives. And yet—"

"Ah, my dear nephew, I know what you would say. I know that the world would embrace such as these within its elastic band as among genuine unselfish workers, though avowedly on a lower level than that adopted by the true Christian. But, after all, can God, the searcher of hearts, approve of anything as being truly unselfish which does not bear the stamp of the Cross? and can anything of which he does not approve be a reality?"

"I suppose not," said the other reluctantly. "Still, it is difficult not to be dazzled by what looks like a reflection from the true Light; and difficult, too, to detect a sham where we are willing to see a reality."

"Very difficult," replied Colonel Dawson; "and yet the world abounds in shams, and cant, and hypocrisy. The world commonly lays these things at the door of religious professors; but the truth all the while is that the sham, and the cant, and the hypocrisy are really in those who take or gain credit for a character unselfishness, for example which is only to be found in true Christians, and hold themselves back from that genuine devotion, and self sacrifice, and coming out to Christ, without which their boasted and lauded excellences are nothing better than a delusion and an empty name."

The young man did not reply, and the subject was dropped for the remainder of the ride home.

VI.

Duty.

MARY STANSFIELD and Grace Willerly were sitting together, about three weeks after the above conversation, in an arbour in the garden attached to Lady Willerly's house. Miss Stansfield had come to spend a day or two by special invitation, by way of getting a little change, which she much needed; her aunt having spared her without a murmur, and having accepted the services of a former domestic in her place.

"How very kind of your aunt to spare you!" said Grace to her friend; "I hardly expected it, knowing how much she depends upon you."

"Oh yes!" was the reply; "you cannot tell,

dear Grace, what a wonderful change has come over my dear aunt. And it is all owing, under God, to the loving faithfulness of our kind friend Colonel Dawson. I scarcely ever get a harsh word or a hard look now; and when I do, my aunt at once calls me to her, and asks me to forgive her. Oh, is it not wonderful? I am sure I blush with shame to think how little I deserve it."

"Yes, it is very wonderful, dear Mary. Certainly our new neighbour is a most earnest and useful man; and he has shown his discernment, too, in getting hold of yourself to work for him in Bridgepath. But I am afraid you will find it very up hill work; you'll want the strength of a horse, the patience of Job, and the zeal of an apostle in such a place as that."

"Certainly, I shall want the grace of an apostle," said the other quietly; "but the work is very delightful, and is more than repaying me already for any little trouble or self denial it may cost me."

"It is very good of you to say so, Mary; I am afraid the work wouldn't suit me. I don't mind making sacrifices indeed, I think I can truly say it is one of my chief pleasures to make them; but there must be something very depressing in the jog trot sort of work you are called on to do. I don't mind anything, so long as it has a little bit of dash in it; but I am afraid I should soon grow weary of a regular grind like yours."

"Oh, but you are quite mistaken about my work at Bridgepath," said the other, laughing. "There is nothing dull or monotonous about it; and it is such a happiness to see the light of God's truth beginning to dawn on dark and troubled hearts. And there is one particularly interesting family I mean John Price's. You have heard, I dare say, that he was steward to the squire, and that he lost almost everything by his poor master's extravagance. Poor man, he is bed ridden now, and I fear had little comfort even from his Bible, for he seemed to have learned little from it but patience. But, oh! how he has brightened up, and his wife and daughter, too, now that they have been led to see that it is their privilege to work and suffer *from* salvation instead of *for* salvation."

"I don't understand you,' interrupted Miss Willerly.

"Don't you? Oh, it makes all the difference. Poor John Price has been reading his Bible, and bearing his troubles patiently, in the hope that at the end he may be accepted and saved through his Saviour's merits. That is what I mean by working *for* salvation."

"And what else, dear Mary, would you have him do?"

"O Grace! this is poor work indeed, working in view of a merely possible salvation. No! what he has learned now is to see that his Saviour, in whom he humbly and truly believes, has given him a present salvation; so that he, and his wife and daughter too, can now say, 'We love him, because he first loved us.' And so they work and suffer cheerfully, and even thankfully, from love to that Saviour who has already received them as his own. This is what I mean by working *from* salvation. Surely we shall work more heartily for one of whom we know that he *has* saved us, than for one of whom we know only that he has saved others, and may perhaps save us also in the end."

"I see what you mean, dear Mary, but I never saw it so before. Such a view of God's love to us personally must take the selfishness out of our good works, because what we do will be done just simply from love to Christ. It is a beautiful way of looking at God's dealings with us."

"Yes, Grace; and as true and scriptural as it is beautiful. It is just what God sees that we need, and furnishes us with the most constraining motive to serve him, and to deny self in his service."

"I see it," said Miss Willerly sadly and thoughtfully, after a pause. "I very much fear, dear Mary, that I have been greatly deceiving myself. I have been just simply building up a monument to my own honour and glory out of my heap of little daily crosses."

"Nay, dear Grace, you are dealing too severely with yourself."

"No, I think not. At any rate, I am sadly aware that not the love of Christ, but the love of human applause, has been the constraining motive in my acts of self-denial. I have made such a parade of my willingness to thwart my own will that I might please others, so that while I should have been startled to see a full-grown trumpeter at my side proclaiming my unselfishness, I have all the while been keeping in my service a little dwarf page, who has been sounding out my praises on his shrill whistle."

"You judge yourself hardly, dear Grace; and yet, no doubt, self does enter largely even into our unselfishness. I am sure I have felt it, oh, how deeply! and specially just lately, since I have undertaken this work at Bridgepath."

"You, dear Mary!"

'Yes, indeed. And I see now how wisely our heavenly Father ordered his discipline in my case. There was indeed a 'needs be' in my dear aunt's former harshness and irritability to me; but for that, and for her disparaging remarks on my conduct, I might have been more self seeking than I am. But the discipline has been changed now, and I trust that the chastisement has not been wholly in vain. What we all want, I am sure, if we are to be true workers for God, is to lift our eyes from self, and keep them steadily fixed on Him who has done so much for us."

"I am sure you are right," said the other. "I know I wish to do right, and I feel a pleasure in crossing my own inclination when it will gratify others; but then my inmost look has been to the world and its approbation. 'What will people say? what will people think?' or, at any rate, 'What will good people say and think?' this has been the prominent thought in my heart, I fear."

"Well, dear Grace, I suppose this is so, more or less, with us all. What we want, I think, and comparatively seldom find in these showy and surface days, is a high sense of duty, so that we just act as duty calls, let the world, or good people even, judge of us or speak of us as they please."

"And yet, dear Mary, I think I see a little crevice through which self may creep in even there. I have met some of your 'duty' people who have flung themselves so violently against the prejudices of society, or, at any rate, of good people, crying out all the time, 'Duty, duty! it don't matter to us what the world thinks,' that they have given great offence where they might have avoided giving any, and have set up people's backs against what is good and true."

"I dare say you have met such, dear Grace, and I think you may be talking to one of the class now," said Miss Stansfield, laughing; "at least, my character and principles would naturally lead me in that direction, for, of course, we are all disposed to carry out our own views to an extreme. if we do not let common sense, enlightened by grace, preserve a proper balance. But, spite of this, I still feel that a high sense of duty in those who love our Saviour is the surest preservative against being carried away by a subtle selfishness. and is the making of the finest and most truly self-denying characters. If I am manifestly in the path of duty, what matters it what is said of me, or who says it? I may then go forward, not, indeed, arrogantly or defiantly — that would be unlike the great Master—but yet firmly and confidently, and God will set me right with the world and with his people in his own good time."

"Ah! I believe you are right," said her friend, with a sigh. " I wish there were more of such true unselfishness amongst us; I wish I were such a character myself."

"And so you are, dear Grace, in the main. No one can possibly doubt your genuineness and sincerity. You have only just to step up on to the higher platform, and, as your heart's gaze becomes more fixed on a Saviour known and loved, you will cease to think about how your self-denial looks in the eyes of others, and will feel the cross which you carry after Christ in the path of duty to be easy and his burden light."

"I shall not forget our conversation on this subject," said Miss Willerly with tears in her eyes. "I always thought that I hated selfishness, but now I see that I have been blinded to my own. I suppose it is very difficult for us to see it in ourselves as it really is, especially in these days when there are so many attractive forms of self denial. It occurred to me the other day what an odd thing it would be to see how a number of utterly selfish people would get on if thrown together for some weeks, with not a single unselfish person amongst them, and unable to get rid of one another's company. I feel sure the result would teach an admirable lesson on the misery of a thoroughly selfish disposition.'

'I think so too, Grace,' said her companion, much amused. "What do you say to putting a story or allegory together on the subject?'

"Capital!" cried Miss Willerly, "it will be something quite in my line. I will set about it at once. I shall be able to give myself some very seasonable raps on the knuckles as I go on, and perhaps I may be of use to some of my acquaintance, who might be induced to look through my performance in a friendly way.'

"You must let me be the first to see it," said her friend

"Oh, certainly; and you must give me your free and candid criticisms."

"Yes, I will do so; and I don't doubt I shall find profit in the reading of it, and a little bit of myself in more than one of your characters."

A fortnight after this conversation Miss Stansfield received from her friend the promised story, which we give in the following chapter.

VII.

The Selfish Islands.

A CERTAIN Eastern despot, whose attention had been painfully drawn to the odious character of selfishness, by finding it exhibited in a very marked manner towards himself by some who had, in looking after their own interests, ventured to thwart the royal will, was resolved to get rid of all the most selfish people out of his capital. To that end he made proclamation that on a certain day he would give a grand banquet to all the *un*selfish people in the metropolis, nothing being needed for admittance to the feast but the personal application of any one laying claim to unselfishness to the lord chancellor for a ticket.

The king took this course under the firm conviction that all the most selfish people, being utterly blinded by self esteem to their own failing, would be the very persons most ready to claim admittance to the banquet; and in this expectation he was not disappointed. But he was a little staggered to find that about a thousand persons, of both sexes and of nearly all ages, applied at the office for tickets of admission and many of them such as had not made their appearance in public for many long years past. Thus, when the feast day came, bed ridden men and women arrived at the palace dressed out in silks and satins; gouty men hobbled in without their crutches; and multitudes who had long been incapacitated from doing anything but try the patience of their friends and indulge their own whims, made no difficulty of appearing among the guests. And it was strange, too, to see at the king's table delicate ladies and chronic invalids, who were never met with at places of worship or benevolent meetings, because the cold or the heat, or their nerves or their lungs made it a duty for them to be keepers at home. There were also present about two hundred spoilt children, whose mothers considered them to be "dear unselfish little darlings," and about an equal number of young ladies and young gentlemen, whose chief delight had consisted in spending their fathers' money, and studying their own sweet persons in the looking-glass.

Of course, the company behaved with due decorum at the banquet, especially as the king did them the honour of sitting down to table with them, the only exception being on the part of the spoilt children, whom not even the presence of royalty itself could restrain from personal encounters over the more attractive-looking dishes.

The banquet over, the king rose and thus addressed his astonished guests:

"I have ascertained from my lord chancellor, whose secretary took down the names and addresses of you all when you applied for your tickets, that he has made careful inquiry into your several characters, and finds that you all belong to a class of persons who greatly trouble our city. You have accepted my invitation professedly as unselfish people, but your estimate of yourselves is the very reverse of that which is held by those who know you best. I have therefore resolved, for the good of the community generally, to transport the whole of you, for a period of six months, to the unin habited island of Comoro, situate in the midst of the great lake, where you will find ample means for living in health, peace, and comfort, provided you are all and each willing to lay aside your selfishness, and to find your happiness in living for the good of others. And I trust that at the end of the six months, when steamers shall call for you at Comoro, you may all be spared to return to your homes improved in character, more useful members of society, and more fitted to contribute to the real prosperity of this kingdom."

Without waiting for a reply, which was not indeed attempted by any of the guests for they remained for some moments speechless with amazement—the king retired from the banqueting hall; and the lord chancellor, motioning with his hand for attention, proceeded to state that each of the guests would be expected to be at the station on a day and at an hour specified on a ticket which each would receive; and that every one would be allowed to take with him or her a reasonable but limited amount of personal luggage, but no furniture or heavy and bulky articles. Steamers would be in readiness, at the Lakeside Terminus, to convey the passengers and their goods to the island; and, as no one would be permitted to decline the journey for all knew that the king's will was law the guests would best consult their own interests and comfort by preparing for the removal with as little delay as possible.

Having made this statement, the lord chancellor withdrew, leaving the company staring one at another in blank dismay. What was to be done? Nothing but to make the best of it; as for resistance, all knew that it would be useless, and remonstrance equally so. Even the infirm and sickly could hope for no exemption; for as their maladies had not hindered their attendance at the banquet, these could not be now admitted as a plea for excusing them from the removal. Many, indeed, of the young people were highly delighted with the prospect before them, especially the children, who were anxious to be off for Comoro there and then. As for their elders, they retired from the palace with varied feelings; some indignant, some conscience stricken, and most prepared to lay the blame on some one or more of their neighbours. Indeed, two old gentlemen, who had been lodgers on different floors in the same house for years, but, in consequence of an old quarrel, had never spoken to one another for the greater part of that time, now blocked up one of the exits from the palace, as they stood face to face, furiously charging each other with being the guilty cause of the terrible calamity which had now fallen on themselves and on so many of their fellow-citizens.

And now the day of departure had arrived, and the trains for the lake were duly filled with passengers; not, however, till many heart-rending scenes had occurred in connection with the luggage. Two young ladies, bosom friends, having hired a van to convey their joint wardrobe and other ornamental effects to the station, were informed, to their tearful despair, that only about one-tenth of the goods could be conveyed to the island. Similarly, three or four fast young men entered the train in a state of desperation bordering on collapse, because the officials had peremptorily turned back a stud of hunters and half a-dozen sporting dogs. But the most exciting scene of all occurred in the case of an old maiden lady, who, having brought a cart-load of personal necessaries and comforts, which were positively essential to her continued existence, and having been firmly refused the transmission of the greater part of them, declared with the utmost positiveness that the lord chancellor had himself expressly informed all the guests at the banquet that each was at liberty to take an *un*limited quantity of goods; nor could any explanation convince her of her mistake. Let them say what they pleased, she had heard the word *un*limited with her own ears; and hearing was believing. The last case which caused any serious difficulty, and which really excited the pity of the porters, was that of an elderly gentleman unfortunate enough to be troubled with a liver, who changed various colours when informed that he must leave behind him an iron bound box containing some four or five hundredweight of patent and other medicines.

At length, all the trains having reached the Lakeside Terminus, the entire party of temporary exiles were duly and speedily conveyed in steamers to the island of Comoro, where they were put on shore with their goods.

The climate of the island was delightful, and subject to but few variations, so that nothing was to be feared by the new comers from inclemency of weather. Care had been also taken by the lord chancellor, to whom the carrying out of the details had been committed, that a sufficient number of tents should be ready for the use of those who chose to avail themselves of them, while building materials and tools had been duly provided, as well as an ample store of provisions.

When the last steamer had discharged its passengers and cargo, proclamation was made by a herald that a commissioner from the king would visit Comoro once a month, to hear any complaints and record any misconduct; and that those who should be found guilty of any grave offence would receive condign punishment at the close of the term of banishment.

The community was then left to follow its own devices. And what would these be? Of course the obvious thing was for each to look after "number one," but he soon became painfully conscious that he could not do this without the help of "number two," and that to obtain this help he must be willing to do his own part. One gentleman, indeed, apparently entirely unconscious of any other duty than that of taking care of himself, set to work at once to make himself as comfortable as circumstances would permit. Having selected the most roomy and convenient tent he could find, he removed his most easily portable possessions into it, and proceeded to regale himself on some cold provisions which he had brought with him.

After these were finished, he rang violently several times a hand bell which he had brought with him, expecting that his valet would at once answer the summons; but he soon found that he could not calculate on his servant's attendance in Comoro. It was true that the man had come on the same steamer as his master, having been one of the guests at the royal banquet; but he had no thought now of looking after any one but himself, and was, when his master rang for him, busily engaged in a drinking bout with a few like minded companions.

And what could the females do? The spoilt children had, of course, their mothers with them—for none but selfish mothers would spoil their children and these mothers with their little ones were preparing to form themselves into a distinct community; but such a frightful contention and uproar arose amongst the children themselves, that before nightfall their parents had to abandon their original idea and seek separate homes among their neighbours. As for the young ladies, they soon managed to enlist the services of the female domestics who had come to the island, and then placed themselves under the protection of two elderly maiden sisters, on the express understanding that their guardians were to be handsomely remunerated for looking after them.

The young gentlemen, having no intention to exert themselves unnecessarily, lounged about with cigars in their mouths, and voted the whole thing "a bore;" while several of the elders of both sexes, suppressing for the time the exhibition of their specialities of selfishness, indulged in a prolonged chorus of grumbling and mutual condolence. But, in one way or other, all had been fed and housed before midnight, and sleep buried for a while in forgetfulness the troubles of the bewildered settlers on Comoro.

We pass over the first month, and how does the commissioner, on his arrival at the island, find the exiles bearing their lot? Proclamation was at once made that those who had anything to complain of should meet him in a spacious marquee which he had caused to be set up on a large open piece of ground near the shore, immediately on his arrival. He was rather dismayed, however, when he found the place of hearing crowded without a moment's delay by nine tenths of the islanders, while many were clamouring outside because unable to obtain admission. After a few moments' consideration, he ordered his officers to clear the marquee, and then to admit a hundred of the more elderly of each sex. This was done with some considerable difficulty, and the commissioner then addressed himself to a crabbed looking old gentleman, who had elbowed his way to the front with a vigour hardly to have been looked for in one of his years and apparent infirmities.

"May I request, sir, to be informed what it is you have to complain of?" asked the commissioner.

"I complain of everything and everybody," was the reply

"Is that *all* you have to complain of?" the commissioner then asked. Before the old gentleman could frame an answer to this second question, the judge, having paused to give a few moments for reply, exclaimed, " Officer, dismiss this complainant;" and the old man was forthwith removed from the tent in a state of boiling indignation.

"And now, madam," continued the commissioner, addressing a middle-aged lady of dignified mien and commanding stature, "may I ask what is your complaint?"

"I complain, sir," replied the lady sternly, "of general neglect and ill treatment."

"Excuse me, madam," was the judge's reply, "but I can see no evidence of this in your personal appearance. So far from it, that, having met you not unfrequently in the streets of our city, I am constrained to congratulate you on the manifest improvement in health which you have gained from a month's residence in this delightful climate.—Officer, conduct this lady with all due ceremony to the outside of our court."

"And you, sir," speaking to a gentleman of very severe countenance, who had been used at home to "show his slaves how choleric he was, and make his bondmen tremble,"—" let me hear what charge you have to allege."

"Charge, Mr. Commissioner! charge enough, I'm sure! Why, I can't get any one to mind a word that I say."

"Then, I am sure, sir, the fault must be wholly or for the most part your own. Officer, remove him."

"Has no one anything more definite to complain of?" he again asked, looking round the assembly, which by this time had begun to thin, as it became obvious to all present that no attention would be given to mere vague grumblings.

"I'm sure it's very hard," sighed a knot of young ladies, who had listened from the outside to what had been going on, and were afraid to speak out more plainly. "We shall be moped to death if we're kept here any longer," muttered one or two fast young men, shrugging their shoulders. But to these remarks the commissioner turned a deaf ear, and no one coming forward to lodge any distinct charge against another, the court broke up, and the commissioner proceeded to make a tour of inspection among the islanders.

He found, as he had indeed expected to find, that the necessity for exertion, and the peculiarity of the circumstances in which they were now placed, had already got rid of a good deal of the selfishness which had only formed a sort of crust over the characters of many who, in the main, were not without kind and generous feelings; so that the looking after the due supply of provisions, and the cooking of them and serving them to the different families, had been cheerfully undertaken by a duly organized body of young and middle aged workers of both sexes, the result of which was, not only an improvement in character in the workers themselves, but also a drawing forth of expressions of gratitude from some who formerly took all attentions as a right, but now had been made to feel their dependence on their fellows. And it was pleasant to see how cordially working men and women were united in striving for the good of the community in conjunction with those who had hitherto occupied a higher social position than themselves.

Some, indeed, of the lower orders, whose tastes had been of an utterly low and degraded cast, had been summarily ejected from the island after they had more than once endangered the lives and stores of the islanders in their brutal drunken sprees. They had talked big, indeed, and made at first a show of resistance; but the general body of the exiles had authorized a powerful force of young and middle aged men to take them into custody, and convey them on a raft, constructed for the purpose, to an island some ten miles distant. Here the rioters were left with a sufficient supply of provisions; a warning being given them that, should they attempt to return to Comoro, they would be put in irons, and kept in custody till they could be brought up before the commissioner. The island being thus happily rid of this disturbing element, there was, at any rate, outward peace among the inhabitants of Comoro, though, of course, there was yet abundance of discontent and bitterness beneath the surface in the hearts of many.

As the commissioner was making his way to the shore preparatory to his return to the mainland, he passed a tent from which there issued such deep fetched sighs that, having obtained permission to enter, he inquired of the inmate the cause of so much trouble.

"Ah, sir!" replied the poor sufferer, who was a man some sixty years of age, with gray hair, and a countenance whose expression was one of mingled shrewdness, discontent, and ill-temper, " our sovereign little knows the cruelty he has been guilty of in sending me all alone to a place like this."

"How alone, my friend?" asked the other; "you have plenty of companions within reach."

" Why, sir," was the poor man's reply, " I have been torn from the best and most loving of wives—I who am so entirely dependent on her for my happiness I who love her so tenderly; alas! wretched man that I am, what shall I do?"

"Do you know this gentleman?" said the

commissioner, turning to his secretary, who had accompanied him into the tent.

"I know him well, your excellency," was the reply; "and a more selfish man does not exist. He tells the truth, however, when he says that he is entirely dependent on his wife for his happiness; but it was impossible for her to accompany him hither, as she is the most unselfish of women. On her he has ever made it a practice to vent his chief spleen and bitterness, exacting from her at the same time perpetual service, and rarely repaying her with anything but sneers and insults, holding her up even to the scorn and ridicule of his acquaintance."

As the secretary uttered these words, a burning blush covered the face of the unhappy man, who ceased his sighs and bent his head upon his hands.

"My friend," said the commissioner gently, "I am truly sorry for you; but I am in hopes that your solitude will work for your good. Think over the past with contrition, and be up and joining in some useful work for the good of others; and when you return home, treat your injured, long-suffering, and admirable wife as a human being, a lady, a companion, a friend, an equal, and not, as you have hitherto done, like a slave or a brute beast."

There was no reply, and the commissioner hastened to the shore. He was about to step into the boat that was to convey him to the steamer, when a young man of dandified appearance and affected manner requested to know whether he could have one moment's private interview with the commissioner before his departure.

"Well, sir," said the other, somewhat impatiently, "you must be brief for I am anxious to lose no time, as business matters at home are pressing."

"Sir," said the young man, dropping, at the same time, his affected drawl, "my case is a hard one, and I would ask if you could not grant me a passage home in the vessel by which you are returning."

"On what grounds?" asked the commissioner.

"Why, sir, I have an old mother and a sister,

both in infirm health, who can hardly get on without me; and it is only just that I should be allowed to return, as my mother, who is a widow, has no other son."

"Do you know this young man?" inquired the commissioner, turning to his secretary.

"Far too well, your excellency; he is the clog of his home, the laughing stock of his companions behind his back, and is despised by all wise and sensible people. He has had situation after situation offered him, in which he could have earned an honest and respectable livelihood, but he has declined one after another as not to his taste. He is far too much of a gentleman, in his own estimation, to enter upon any work that will involve any steady exertion; but he does not scruple to sponge upon his poor mother, to whose support he contributes nothing, and who has barely enough to meet her own needs, while he borrows—that is, appropriates—the savings of his delicate sister, who, though in feeble health, has undertaken tuition, because this brother of hers is too fine a gentleman to live in anything but idleness, and spends those hard-earned savings of hers as pocket-money on his own elegant pleasures and follies."

"Contemptible wretch!" exclaimed the commissioner with flashing eyes; "stay where you are, and learn, if it is possible, by the end of these six months, to see that you have a duty to others as well as to your own despicable self."

Amazed at this exposure and reply, the young man dropped his eye-glass from his eye, and his cigar from his mouth, and stood staring in bewilderment at the commissioner as he sprang into the boat and made for the steamer which was to convey him home.

Only one other incident worth recording happened during the commissioner's subsequent visits; for the discipline involved in their banishment had produced the good result of making the various exiles feel the necessity of bearing and forbearing, giving and taking, and of each doing his and her part in contributing to the comfort and happiness of the whole. The incident referred to happened during the commissioner's third monthly visit.

Soon after his arrival he received a respectful note from the secretary of a Ladies' Working Committee, requesting him to receive a deputation from their society at the place of audience. This request having been graciously acceded to, and the deputation received by his excellency in due form, the spokeswoman of the party, a young lady in spectacles, expressed the conviction, on behalf of herself and companions, that a sad but no doubt unintentional mistake had been made by his majesty in including themselves in the party sent to Comoro. They were associated, and had been so for years past, as workers together for many benevolent objects and therefore this sending of them to the "Selfish Island" was a double wrong; for it not only threw a slur on their society, whose members were banded together for the purpose of working for the good of others, but it also deprived many suffering ones at home of the help and comfort they had been used to derive from the united and self-denying efforts of these their true and loving friends.

The commissioner having listened with due politeness and attention to this address, assured the deputation that the king would be sorry to have done them any wrong, should such prove to have been the case, and that he would duly report the matter to his majesty. He could not, however, release them on the present occasion; but he hoped, after having made full inquiry into the case on his return, that he should be able to bring them, on his next monthly visit, the welcome permission to leave the island.

Having returned to Comoro in due time, his first care was to request the Ladies' Working Committee to meet him again by deputation. This was accordingly done, and the commissioner addressed them as follows:—

"I exceedingly regret, ladies, that I cannot promise you any shortening of your time of banishment. His majesty has received your complaint, and has caused due investigation to be made; and the result of that investigation has not led him to make any relaxation in your case. For it has been clearly ascertained that the good works and charitable deeds of which you informed me on my last visit, consisted in your attending to work to which you were not called, to the neglect of duties which plainly belonged to you; and that for any seeming sacrifice you made in the bestowal of your time and labour, you more than repaid yourselves in the applause which you managed to obtain from a troop of ignorant or interested admirers. It would, in fact, appear that your benevolence and labour for others involved no real self-denial in it, but was only, after all, another but less obvious form of selfishness. His majesty admires and respects nothing more than genuine co-operation in working for the benefit of the suffering and the needy; but in your case this stamp of genuineness is found to be wanting. We trust, however, that your present work may prove to be of a better character, and that at the expiry of your exile you will return home prepared to do good from truly pure and unselfish motives."

Murmurs followed, as they had accompanied, this speech, but the commissioner was inexorable.

And now at last the six months had come to an end, and the exiles of Comoro flocked to the steamers which were to convey them back to the mainland. The discipline had been with most very salutary. Roughing it for the first time in their lives had been the means with many of smoothing out the wrinkles of grosser selfishness from their characters. Others had learned to look at things through their neighbours' eyes, and thus had come to think less about themselves and about consulting their own pleasure merely. Some also who had moved up and down in a groove all their previous lives, and had made all about them miserable or uncomfortable by their unbending and ungracious habits, had learned the wisdom, and happiness, too, of bending aside a little from the path of their own prejudices to accommodate a neighbour. Many likewise, having been forced to do things of which, on their first landing on Comoro, they had loudly proclaimed themselves physically incapable, now found, to no one's surprise so much as their own, that their former impossibilities could henceforth be performed by themselves with ease. While a few, who had been in the habit of glorying in unselfishness as their strong point, had come to detect their own weakness when they got little or no credit from their neighbours for their ambitious acts of self denial. And one thing was specially worthy of remark, so far from suffering in health, every one returned home greatly improved in looks and vigour by this compulsory stay in the clear and bracing atmosphere of Comoro. As for the hypochondriacal gentleman, who had felt so keenly the refusal to be allowed to take his packing case of medicines with him, he had returned in such a state of spirits that he at once sold his extensive stock of drugs by auction, and gave the money to an hospital for incurables. And, indeed, so great was the gain to the metropolis, in the first place by the absence of the exiles, and afterwards by their altered character, for the most part, on their return to their homes, that the king, when talking over the matter with the commissioner, whom he had selected for the post as, by general acknowledgment, the most upright, downright, straightforward, honest-minded man in his kingdom,—declared that he should like to try the atmosphere of Comoro himself some day, as it was proved to be so healthy and improving.

"I most heartily advise your majesty to do so," said the commissioner, somewhat bluntly; "and if your majesty will only take the entire cabinet with you, I have little doubt but that the benefit to yourself and your ministers will be most heartily acknowledged and thoroughly appreciated by your subjects on your majesty's auspicious return."

VIII.

A Little Mysterious.

MARY STANSFIELD pursued her quiet work at Bridgepath amongst the poor, being welcomed by all, but by none so cordially as by John Price and his family, who seemed quite different people now from what they used to be. And why? Just because they had exchanged resignation for God's peace. Their characters and conduct were outwardly the same; but there was a new light in them and reflected from them, even the light that shines in hearts where Jesus dwells as a Saviour known and loved, a light which brightens the heavy clouds of earthly sadness and spans them with a rainbow of immortal hope. And not only so, but, in consequence of the entrance of this purer light, a change for the better was taking place in the bodily health of the poor bed-ridden man for a wounded spirit had had a good deal to do with his physical infirmities so that there seemed a likelihood that he would be able in time to leave his sick-bed and go forth once more, not indeed to laborious work, but to fill some light post which the colonel had in store for him.

It was on a lovely afternoon that he was sitting up in his arm chair, dressed in clothes which he had never thought to put on again. He was listening to the gentle but earnest voice of Mary Stansfield, as she read to him from the Word of God, and spoke a few loving and cheering words of her own upon the passage she had selected. A shadow fell across her book; she looked up. The colonel and his nephew stood in the open doorway.

"Don't let us interrupt you, Miss Stansfield," said the former; "I was only looking round with my nephew, who has not been here before, to see how things are going on in Bridgepath. We will call again'

They passed on, and Miss Stansfield resumed her reading. But somehow or other John Price's attention seemed to wander—he looked disturbed, and fidgeted in his chair; and so his visitor, thinking that he had been read to as long as he could hear with comfort and profit in his weak state, closed the book, and rose to leave.

"Oh, don't go, miss!" cried the old man in a distressed voice. "I'm so sorry; but something as I can't exactly explain just took away my thoughts and troubled me when the colonel came to the door. But go on, go on, miss; I'm never tired of hearing the good news from your lips."

"No, John," replied Miss Stansfield; "I think we shall do for to-day. You are not strong enough yet to bear much strain of mind or body; and Colonel Dawson will be coming in directly, and will like to have a word with you, and so, I am sure, will Mr. Horace; so I will say good-bye."

The other looked scared and bewildered, and made no reply. "Poor John!" said his kind visitor to herself, as she left the cottage and went on her way; "I am afraid I have tired him. And yet I think there must be something more than that which troubles him."

A few minutes later the colonel and his nephew entered John Price's house. "Come in, Horace," said Colonel Dawson; "you have not yet been introduced to one who will, I hope, be spared to be a great helper in the good work in Bridgepath, though he does not look much like a worker at present. But the Lord has been doing great things for him already, and, I doubt not, means to do greater things for him yet."

The young man stepped forward up to the old man's chair, and held out his hand to him. John Price grasped it eagerly with both his own thin, wasted hands, and looking at him with a half-astonished, half distressed gaze, said abruptly, in a hoarse, choking voice, "What's your name?"

"My name?" said the young man, smiling at his earnestness. "My name, old friend, is Horace Jackson."

"Horace Horace!" muttered the other in a tone of great excitement; "it must be—nay, it cannot be and yet it must be. Are you sure, sir, your name's Jackson?"

The young man, surprised at such a question, was about to reply, when the colonel, coming forward, stooped over the old man and whispered a few words in his ear. The poor invalid immediately sank back in his chair, and covered his eyes with his hand for a moment; then he sat up again, and took part in the conversation, but in a dreamy sort of way, keeping his face steadily turned away from his younger visitor. But as the colonel and his nephew were leaving the cottage, he fixed upon the latter a look so full of anxiety and interest, that it was quite clear that Horace Jackson had opened unwittingly a deep spring of feeling in John Price's heart, which the old man found it almost impossible to repress. As his visitors retired, Colonel Dawson, looking back, put his finger on his lips, to which sign John Price slowly bent his head.

In a few minutes the colonel returned alone.

"I have left my nephew at the school," he said, "to give the children a questioning on what they have been lately learning; and now, John, I shall be able to clear up your doubts and fears, and to set your mind at rest on a subject which I see affects you deeply." A long and interesting communication was then made by the colonel to his humble friend, at the close of which the invalid seemed as if he could have sprung out of his chair for very gladness, while the tears poured from his eyes, and his lips murmured words of thankfulness.

As Colonel Dawson was leaving, he turned and said with a smile, "Remember, John, not a word to any one at present not till I give you leave."

"All right, sir; you may depend upon me. The Lord be praised!" was the reply; and as the old man said the words, every wrinkle in his careworn face seemed running over with light. But for the present Horace Jackson did not call at his cottage again, though he now and then appeared in the village, and was to be seen on more than one occasion accompanying Miss Stansfield on her return from Bridgepath.

And now it began to be rumoured about in the neighbourhood that an attachment was springing up between the colonel's nephew and Mary Stansfield; and all true hearted people rejoiced, knowing what a blessing the union of two such earnest workers would prove, as, of course, they would one day, if spared, succeed to the Riverton estate. The world, however, was both surprised and disgusted, having hoped "better things" of the young man. As for the Wilders, they were full of dark and bitter sayings on the subject the younger Mr. Wilder especially, who was never tired of remarking to his acquaintance, when the subject was broached, that "Miss Stansfield had contrived to play her cards well." This observation was not lost on the busy bodies and scandal mongers who abounded in Franchope, as they do in most country towns, where there is not so much of active business stirring as will furnish sufficient material for gossip to those who love to act as unpaid news-agents in publishing their neighbours' real or supposed more private doings from house to house.

There happened to live at the outskirts of the little town an elderly lady possessed of singular activity in all her members, especially that most unruly one, the tongue. Give her a little bit of local news or a hard saying to report, and she would never rest till she had distributed the information throughout her entire acquaintance, with a little garnish of her own to the savoury dish, according to the taste or appetite of her hearers. Loved by none, feared by all, her calls were received with apparent cordiality, partly from a natural relish in many for questionable news, and partly from a desire to stand well with one who had the reputations of her neighbours and associates more or less in her power. Young Wilder's remark on Miss Stansfield's engagement was a choice morsel of scandal to old Mrs. Tinderley, and was duly reported in every house to which she had access. But that was not all. Meeting Mary Stansfield herself one day near her aunt's house, Mrs. Tinderley grasped her warmly by the hand—though hitherto they had never done more than just exchange civil greetings by word of mouth and congratulated her upon her happy prospects. Miss Stansfield, who knew the old lady's character well, was about to pass on, after a word or two of civil acknowledgment, but the other would not let her part from her so hastily.

"My dear," she exclaimed in an earnest half-whisper, "isn't it really shameful that people should say the ill natured things they do, calling you a hypocrite, and selfish of all things in the world? And young Mr. Wilder too to think of his saying that 'you've played your cards well.' Really, it's too bad. But, my dear Miss Stansfield, if I were you I wouldn't mind it."

The old lady paused, expecting to see a blush of vexation and annoyance on her young companion's face; but she was disappointed.

"Thank you, Mrs. Tinderley," replied Mary Stansfield, "I suppose you mean well by repeating to me these foolish remarks. I can assure you that I do *not* mind them, as my conscience quite acquits me in the matter, and my happiness in no degree depends on the judgment of those who have made or reported them."

So saying, she went quietly on her way, leaving poor Mrs. Tinderley in a state of utter bewilderment.

To Colonel Dawson the attachment, which was soon avowed on his nephew's part, was a matter of the sincerest satisfaction; as it was also to the elder Miss Stansfield, who had learned to take great pleasure in the society of Horace Jackson, and to see in him those excellences of a true Christian character which would make him a suitable husband to her invaluable niece. She was pained, however, at the hard things which had been said on the subject, as reported to her by an acquaintance of Mrs. Tinderley's, and spoke to the colonel on the subject.

"I am sure, Colonel Dawson," she said, "dear Mary is without blame in this matter. The idea of *her* acting selfishly or 'playing her cards,' such a thing is altogether preposterous.

I cannot imagine how people can be so wicked as to make such cruel and unjust remarks."

"Ah, my dear friend," replied the colonel, smiling, "let it pass, the world will have its say. I am sure your dear niece will have no wish, as I know she has no need, to vindicate her character from such aspersions. She has just gone straight forward in the path of duty, and has met Horace while in that path; and to my mind there would be somewhat of selfishness, or, at any rate, of undue self-consciousness, on her part were she to trouble herself, or to allow her friends to trouble themselves, to defend her conduct in this matter. We are, of course, as Christians, to abstain from all appearance of evil, and to give no handle to the enemies of the truth against us or our profession; but it does not, therefore, follow that we are to decline a path which plainly opens before us in God's providence, just because that path may be a smooth one, or may lead to a position of wealth and influence. To choose another path which will gain us high credit for self-denial, because we turn away from that which is naturally more attractive to ourselves, may after all be only another though subtler form of selfishness. Surely the right course is just to go in honesty of purpose unreservedly where God's hand is plainly guiding us and he will take care both of our character and of his own cause in connection with that character, as he orders everything else that is really essential to the welfare and usefulness of each of his own dear children "

IX.

Ruby Grigg.

HORACE JACKSON had come to take a deep interest in the inhabitants of Bridgepath, especially since his engagement; for Mary Stansfield's heart was thoroughly in her work in that once benighted place, and she was only too glad to lead one now so dear to her to concern himself in the truest welfare of those in Bridge path who were still living without thought of any world but this.

Things had indeed greatly improved through the diligent and loving exertions of the excellent schoolmaster, who was evidently determined to tread down all opposition that came in his way by the firm and weighty, though gentle, steps of a steady and consistent Christian walk. His task, it is true, was no easy one, for parents and scholars seemed for a time to be in league against all endeavours on his part to remove existing abuses. It was all very right, they allowed, that he should teach the children head knowledge—this they were content to put up with; but as for his influencing the heart, or inducing them to change their conduct, and thereby to give up the pleasures of sin in which they had so long delighted, this was not to be tolerated; they were determined not to submit to it. And so the boys, when they could no longer carry on their encounters and settle their differences with the fist after school without interruption and remonstrance from the master, revenged themselves for this interference with their privileges by a thousand little sly tricks and bits of mischief at his expense, and with the full approbation, or, at any rate, connivance, of their friends.

As for the grown up people generally, they gave the good master and his loving wife to understand, when they paid friendly visits to the parents of the scholars, that the inhabitants of the hamlet could do just as well if left to themselves; that they were too old now to go to school; and as for the master's religious teaching, they had already quite as much religion amongst them as was necessary for their comfort and well being: in fact, the schoolmaster and his wife would best consult their own interests and the peace of the place by being keepers at home and looking after their own household out of school hours.

Nor was this all. The good man having, in one of his Sunday evening addresses in the schoolroom, spoken some very plain though kindly words against sinful courses too prevalent in Bridgepath, an assault was made on his little garden one night during the following week, so that when he looked over his flower-beds next morning he found them all trampled over, his rose trees cut down, and the flower roots torn up and thrown about in all directions.

As he rose from the examination of what remained of a favourite tree his eyes encountered those of one of his most determined opponents in the village. The man was staring over the wall, and when his eyes met those of the schoolmaster, he inquired with a grin how his roses were getting on. With a slight flush on his face, but yet with a smile on his lips, the master replied very slowly, "I shall have to kill some of you for this." Before the evening this little sentence had been reported in every house in Bridgepath.

"So you're a going to kill some of us, master. I thought you was one of them peaceable Christians," sneered a man to the schoolmaster as he was passing by the door of one of the beer-shops, before which a number of men were assembled with their pipes and pots. There was a general scornful laugh at this speech. Nothing dismayed, however, the schoolmaster stood still, and facing his opponent, said, "Yes, I said I would kill some of you, and I mean it; and if you will come up to the schoolroom to-night at eight o'clock, I will tell you all how and why."

"Let's go and hear him," said one of the drinkers. "Ay, let us," said another.

By eight o'clock the schoolroom was half filled with men, women, and children. The master was standing at his desk ready to receive them, and when the school clock had struck the hour, began as follows:

"Now, my friends and neighbours, I feel sure that you'll give me a quiet hearing, as you have come that you may know why I said I must kill some of you. You've done me harm, some of you, but I've done you none; so the least you can do is to listen to me patiently."

"Ay, ay," said one or two voices, and there was a hush of earnest attention.

The master then unlocked his desk, and taking out a printed paper, read it out clearly and with due spirit and emphasis. It was the admirable tract entitled "The Man who Killed his Neighbour." When he had finished reading there was a general murmur of satisfaction, and all were deeply attentive as he went on to say, "Now, dear friends, that's the way I mean to kill some of you; I mean to do it by patience, by kindness, and by returning good for evil, as the good man in the tract did. I'm sorry of course, that my roses have been cut down and my flower-beds trampled on. But let that pass; I shan't fret over it, nor try to find out who did it. But I do want to get you to believe that my great desire and aim is to do you good; and if I can manage, by God's help, to persuade you of this, I shall have killed the enemy that is living in your hearts against me, and we shall be happy and good friends."

No one offered any reply, and the meeting broke up; but the master had gained his object. Many who had been set against him were now thoroughly ashamed of themselves; nearly every door was gladly opened to himself and his wife; and one morning, when he came out into his garden, he found that some unknown hands had planted new rose-trees in the place of those which had been destroyed. So the good man was making a way steadily for the spread of the truth.

Nevertheless, the evil one had still many devoted followers, especially among the tipplers. As one of these unhappy men was one day emerging from a beer-shop in Bridgepath, with flushed face and uncertain step, he ran against Horace Jackson, who was just then passing through the village. Uttering a loud oath, the man was about to move on, when Horace, catching him by the arm, compelled him to stand still, while he sharply reproved him for his drunkenness and profanity. A little staggered and abashed, the man muttered something that sounded half like an apology; and then, shaking himself free from Horace's grasp, pointed with his pipe across the green, and said scoffingly, " 'Tain't of no use speaking to me. If you wants a good hard piece to try your hand on, see what you can do with Ruby Grigg yonder;" saying which, he plunged back into the beer-shop.

Vexed and annoyed at this encounter, Horace was just about to hasten on, when his eyes fell on the man to whom the poor drunkard had referred him; and who was seated not far off on the other side of the green, upon the steps of a large travelling van. The young man's heart died within him as he gazed at the strange uncouth being to whom he was invited to try and do some good.

Reuben Gregson, popularly known as "Ruby Grigg," was anything but a jewel in appearance. He wore at this time a very long coat, whose original colour, whatever it might have been, had now faded into a yellowish dirty brown in those parts which still remained unpatched. Trousers just reaching a little below the knee, and repaired here and there with remnants of staring blue cloth of various shapes and sizes, were succeeded by yellowish gray stockings, and by shoes which, if they ever enjoyed the luxury of blacking, must have last done so at a very remote period. A hat, which had once been black and of some definite shape, but was now rimless, distorted, and of the same faded hue as the coat, being stuck on one side, only partially covered a tangled mass of grayish hair, which radiated wildly in every direction. Beneath the foremost locks were two eyeballs, the one sightless, the other black and piercing, and ever on the move, having to do double duty. A rough, stubbly, and anything but cleanly beard, which was submitted to the razor only on festal occasions, gave an additional wildness to a countenance which was furrowed across the forehead and down either cheek with deep lines blotched and freckled. As for the mouth, it was a perfect study in itself. Usually pretty tightly closed, it displayed when open a small remnant of teeth at irregular intervals, and now grown old and decayed by long service. But, whether open or shut, there was an expression of amused consciousness and cunning about that mouth, as though the owner were living in a chronic state of self satisfaction at having fairly outwitted somebody. Such was Ruby Grigg in his personal appearance.

His caravan, also, was a very original and peculiar structure, manifestly built more for use than ornament, and combining both shop and dwelling. It was formed of boards of various lengths and widths, some painted and others bare, the business part being in front, and arched over with a stout framework which was covered with a tight-fitting tarpaulin; while at the back a square little house, painted uniformly a sober green, and protected by a sloping roof of brown coloured wood-work, and lighted by two little windows, served as parlour, bedroom, and kitchen to Ruby and his wife.

Mrs. Gregson, or Sally Grigg as she was usually styled, was not a noticeable person, keeping out of the way as much as possible; and devoting her time and energies to seeing to the due feeding of her husband, his horse and dog, and herself these forming the entire family, for they had no children and also to taking care of, and tidying up from time to time, the very miscellaneous wares which were offered for sale in the caravan.

Ruby's affections seemed pretty equally divided between his horse, his dog, and his wife the two first having probably the best place in his heart. The horse, like its owner, had no external beauty to boast of, and must have numbered many years since the days of its foalhood. There was something rather knowing about its appearance, as though it had contracted a measure of cunning from constant companionship with its master. The dog, whose name was Grip, was one of those nondescript animals which seem to have inherited a mixture of half-a-dozen different breeds, and had a temper as uncertain as its pedigree. While journeying, his place was beneath the caravan, to which he was attached by a light chain, in which position he was a terror to all who might venture near the caravan without his master's company or permission. When the little party rested for a day or so, Grip had his liberty; which he occasionally abused by appropriating to himself the meals intended for his fellow dogs, none of whom, however superior to him in size or strength, durst for a moment resist him.

Such were the old man and his establishment. His business was that of a miscellaneous salesman, the difficulty being rather to say what he did not than what he did offer to his various customers. The front part of his van was hung with all sorts of hardware, inside and out; but, besides this, there were, within, secret drawers and cupboards containing articles which would not bear exhibition to the public

—such as smuggled goods, both wearable and drinkable, which Ruby knew how to procure at a very low price, and could always part with confidentially for a sum which both suited the pockets of the purchasers, and also brought considerable profit to himself. Among his secret wares were also immoral songs, and impure and infidel books, for which he had many eager buyers, especially in such places as Bridgepath. He had his regular rounds, and his special customers, and was in the habit of attending all the feasts and fairs for many miles round.

It need hardly be said that poor Ruby knew nothing and cared nothing about better things; his heart was wholly in the world, and in making money as fast as he could, by hook or by crook,—and in this he was succeeding. For though the poor man and his wife were utterly godless, and even profane, yet Ruby was no drunkard; he loved his glass, it is true, but he loved money more, and so he always contrived to keep a clear head and a steady eye and hand. He also took good care of his horse and dog for his own sake, as he wanted to make the best and the longest of their services, and was shrewd enough to know that you cannot get out of anything, whether animate or inanimate, more than is put into it. So self and wife, and horse and dog were all well fed and cared for, and worked harmoniously together.

This was the man to whom the poor drunkard pointed his pipe and sneeringly invited Horace Jackson to try and do him good. The young man shrunk at first instinctively from coming in contact with old Reuben. Surely there was abundance of self denying work in looking after the inhabitants of the hamlet itself; why then need he concern himself about a man who was only a passer through, and had no special claim on his attention? Half-satisfied with these thoughts, Horace Jackson was about to proceed homewards, when it seemed to him that a voice, as it were, said within him, "Accept the work; it may not be in vain." Though still reluctant, he now felt that he could no longer hang back; so he crossed the green, and greeted the old hawker kindly.

Ruby looked up at him with a comical twinkle in his one eye, and, knocking out the ashes from his pipe, observed, ' So you be the young gent as is turning all things topsy-turvy in this here village you and the colonel be tween you. I've heard all about it; and a precious mess you'll make of it, I doubt."

"My friend," said Horace, now perfectly relieved from all feeling of disinclination to encounter the old man, "you make a little mistake there: when we came here we *found* things topsy turvy already, and we are just trying, by God's help. to set them upright and straight."

"And I suppose you think as you're going to do it," said the other scornfully.

"Yes, 1 hope so," was the reply. "Come, my friend, now tell me honestly, isn't it happier for the people of this village to have a good school and a good schoolmaster set down amongst them than to be living as they used to do, without proper instruction for the children, and without any knowledge of God and a better world?"

"Can't say as to that," said Ruby Grigg doubtfully, and a little sulkily; "there's lots of people here as likes the old ways better."

"Perhaps so," said Horace; "but they may be wrong in what they like. Now, I ask you again tell me honestly—don't you see a change for the better yourself in Bridgepath?"

"Well, I don't know," replied the old man, fidgeting about; "it's been a worse change for me. I ain't done anything like the business this time as I use doing here, leastways in some things."

Horace had now seated himself by the old man, spite of a deep growl from Grip, whose nearer approach was cut short by a backhanded slap from his master.

"Look there now, old friend," continued the young man. At this moment the school doors were thrown open, and out poured a stream of boys and girls, tumbling one over another in their excitement, and singing gaily as they began to disperse over the green. But all suddenly stopped, for the schoolmaster made his appearance, and all clustered round him. School was over, and what was going to happen now? In former days the sight of the master would have been a signal for every boy and girl to slink out of reach of his observation; but now the master's coming was hailed with a happy shout, and the young ones vied with one another in getting near him, while the youngest clung to his dress, and all looked up at him with bright and happy smiles. Horace turned towards the old man, and marked a flush on his worn and weather-beaten features. "That's a sight worth seeing, my friend," he added; "I think it used not to be so."

Reuben made no answer. His eye seemed to be gazing at something beyond the busy scene before him.

"You've never had any children of your own, it may be," said Horace, noticing his absent look.

Slowly the old man turned towards his

companion, his face was now quite pale, and tears began to steal down its deep furrows. "I've never a child now,' he said in a hoarse and troubled voice, " but I had once a blessed little 'un she were, but she died."

"It may be, friend," said the young man gently, "that the Lord took her in mercy from the evil to come. Did she die very young?"

Reuben Gregson seemed unable to reply for a while, then he said slowly, and apparently with a great effort, "Ay, sir, very young, and she were all the boys and girls I ever had. She were but five year old when she died, but she died happy, poor thing. It's more nor thirty years now since she left us."

"And she died happy, you say?" asked Horace, deeply touched. "Did she know anything of her Saviour?"

"I believe you," replied the other earnestly, "yes. There were a good young lady she ain't living now as seed her playing about by the roadside one day, and gave her this book." Ruby drew out from his breast-pocket a large faded leathern case, and from its inmost depths brought out a small picture-book full of coloured Scripture prints. The frontispiece represented our Saviour hanging on the cross, and was much worn, as with the pressure of little fingers. "There, sir," continued the old man, "the young lady showed her them pictures, and talked to her about 'em, and particular about Him as was nailed to the cross. We was staying on a common near her house for a week or more, and each day that young lady came and had a talk to our little Bessy. And she never forgot what the lady said to her. And so, when she were took with the fever, some weeks arter that, when we was far off from where the lady lived, her last words was, 'Daddy, I'm going to Jesus, 'cos he said, "Suffer the little children to come to me."' There, sir, I've told you now what I haven't spoken to nobody else these thirty years."

"And won't you follow your dear child to the better land?" asked Horace kindly; "there's room in our Saviour's heart and home for you too."

"I don't know, I don't know." said the other gloomily; "these things ain't in my line. Besides, I'm too old and too hard now; it's no use for such as me to think about 'em."

Horace said nothing immediately, but taking out a little New Testament, he read out, without any comment, the parables of the lost sheep and the lost piece of silver. Then he said, "Old friend, I am so glad we have met. Will you accept this little book from me? It will tell you better than I can all about the loving Saviour, who has taken that dear child to himself, and wants you and your wife to follow her."

Without saying a word Ruby clutched the Testament, thrust it into his breast-pocket and then, rising hastily, said, " I wish you good day, sir; maybe we shall meet again. Thank you kindly for the little book."

"Farewell for the present," said Horace. "Yes, I believe we shall meet again," and he turned his steps homewards, deeply thankful that he had not declined the work which was so unexpectedly thrust upon him.

X.
A Rough Jewel Polished.

SOME months had passed since Horace Jackson's brief conversation with Ruby Grigg on the green at Bridgepath, and the good work was making steady progress in that hamlet. A few of the adversaries continued rather noisy and troublesome; but it was observable that these avoided, as by common consent, one particular beer shop, which used to be a favourite resort of the roughest and most dissolute characters, while the publican himself who kept this house was to be seen, at first occasionally, and now regularly at the service which was held in the schoolroom on the Sunday evenings.

News of this happy change had reached Horace from several quarters, and gave the sincerest pleasure to himself and his uncle. Meditating thankfully on these things, the young man was passing one afternoon down a by-lane which led to Bridgepath. It was a lonely spot, far from any house. On either hand the lane was closed in by tall hedges, and a broad belt of turf skirted the rugged road on each side, affording pasture to any stray beasts which might wander thither unbidden. Wild flowers and singing birds filled the untrimmed bushes; while the lowing of cattle, faintly heard from some far-off farm or pasture, added depth to the solitude. With his face turned in the direction of Bridgepath, Horace had just crossed the top of another and narrower lane, which joined at right angles that along which he was walking, and had passed the opening about a hundred yards, when he was startled by hearing a voice behind him shouting out, "Hi! hi! hi! mister!" He looked back, and the sight that met his eye was not reassuring A tall figure, bare-headed and without a coat, was striding after him, tossing its arms about, and brandishing in the right hand a long whip.

The thought at once suggested itself to Horace that this must be some poor lunatic escaped from an asylum, and the idea of a solitary encounter in that lonely spot was not an agreeable one, especially as the young man had no other weapon with him than a thin walking cane, and he was well aware that these poor creatures, when excited and at liberty, often exhibited great strength of limb, and made use of it without scruple to the detriment of any they might fall in with; so he took no heed of the outcry, and hastened his pace onwards. But this had only the effect of exasperating his pursuer, who bawled out to him to stop, and then began to make after him with a shuffling sort of run. So when Horace looked back, and saw the presumed lunatic thus quickening his speed, and also wildly flourishing his whip, he fairly broke into a run himself, considering that, under the circumstances, " discretion was," undoubtedly, " the better part of valour." He was, however, arrested in his flight by a roaring burst of laughter from the supposed madman, which made him pause for a moment and turn full round; and then he became convinced that the cause of his anxiety, who was now leaning his back against a bank, and still laughing vociferously, was none other than the old caravan hawker, Ruby Grigg.

As soon as he could recover himself, the old man began to walk quietly forward, motioning to the other to come and meet him. Horace did this, though with some little reluctance, not feeling sure that the old man's excitement might not be caused by either insanity or drink. But he was soon satisfied that all was right on that score, as the two drew nearer together.

"So you took me for a highwayman or a madman, Mr. Horace!" said the old man, still laughing. "Eh! I don't wonder; you must have thought it very strange. But I never thought how it'd look when I hollered arter you; I were only afeard you'd get out of hearing, and I've something to tell you as'll make your heart right glad, I know."

"What is it, my friend?"

"Well, can you spare me a few minutes, and I'll tell you? My van's just a few yards down the lane you crossed a minute ago. You didn't look that way as you passed, and I didn't take it in at first that it was yourself; and when my wife said. 'There's Mr. Horace Jackson just gone by,' I ran to the top of the lane just as I was, whip and all, and shouted arter you. Can you come with me for a minute?"

"With all my heart," replied the other.

So they turned back, and soon reached the van, which was drawn up by the hedge-side, Grip and the old horse strolling about at leisure, and Mrs. Gregson being engaged in cooking something savoury in an iron pot which was suspended over an open-air fire, gipsy fashion.

When Horace had seated himself on the bank, the old hawker plunged into his travelling shop, and having returned with something in his right hand, seated himself by his young companion. "It's this here little Testament as has been and gone and done it," he said abruptly, opening his hand at the same time and disclosing the book which Horace had given him at their last meeting.

Greatly surprised and touched at these words, Horace looked earnestly into Reuben's face for an explanation, and as he did so, it struck him that the old expression of cunning had given place to one of gentleness and peace.

"I'll tell you all about it, sir,' proceeded the other. "You must know as I haven't been easy in my mind for some time past never since that new schoolmaster at Bridgepath said a few words to me last feast day. You know I often come to the village, 'cos I've some good customers there, and I never used to miss the feast. Well, I'd heard a deal about the new goings on there long afore I set my own eyes on any on 'em, and I weren't best pleased, nor weren't my best customers neither, you may be sure. But still, down in my heart, I couldn't help feeling as things were being changed for the better; yet it didn't quite suit my pocket that they should be, and so I were very cross, and ready to take everything by the wrong handle. So when the schoolmaster came and spoke to me, I were as grumpy at first as a bear with a sore head, as the saying is. But he wouldn't see it—no, not a bit, and talked to me as pleasant as if I'd been all the while looking sugar and honey at him; and I began to feel very uneasy all over. Then, too, I couldn't help seeing as the boys and girls were as different as possible from what they used to be. Many was the time as I've sworn with a big ugly oath as I'd set Grip at them, when they came up and plagued me and wanted to meddle with my goods. But there weren't no need for it now. Yet I stuck out for all that, and talked it over with the keepers of the beer shops; and we all agreed as it were a great nuisance setting up this new school and reading room. But we didn't really think so, except that it began to hurt our trade; for this was where the shoe pinched. And then it was, when my mind was a playing at 'see-saw,' first up on this side, and then up on the other, that you was sent that day to have a talk about the children and my own blessed little 'un, and to give me the Testament. When you was gone, I grumbled to myself at first, 'Precious humbug this! What's the use of a Testament to me? I ain't a-going to pull a long face and sing psalms,' and I were half in the mind to throw it away."

"And what stopped you, old friend?" asked Horace.

"I'll just tell you, sir," replied the other. "When you gave it me, I stuck it in my coat-pocket, next my little girl's picture-book; and when I took it out again, t'other little book came with it, and I couldn't for the life of me do it any harm. So I put 'em both back again side by side; and the next time as we camped in a quiet place, I took the Testament out and began to read a bit out loud. And Sally heard me, and she came and listened with her mouth and eyes wide open, and then asked me what the book was and where I'd got it. I told her all about it; and then she asked me if I thought I could find in the book them last words which our dear little 'un spoke. I told you, sir, you'll remember, as she said, 'Jesus said, "Suffer the little children to come unto me."' Them was her last words, poor thing! Well, we sat on these steps day after day and hunted for them words between us; and we found 'em at last. But we found something else as we hadn't been looking for. We found a couple of miserable old sinners, Ruby and Sally Grigg, as was going along the broad road to destruction." He paused, for his voice had become choked and troubled.

"And did you find nothing more?" asked Horace, deeply interested.

"Ay, to be sure we did, sir. We found Jesus Christ was willing to have us; and we found peace—not at first, nor all at once, but by degrees, and after a while. Sally were the first to get a firm hold: but I believe I've grasped it myself now, and by God's help I mean not to let go."

"This is indeed joyful news, dear friend," said Horace Jackson, when he could trust himself to speak. "Who would have thought it?"

"Ay, who indeed?" said Reuben warmly. "And now," he added, "I want a bit of advice, sir, from you, for it ain't all grass and gravel with me now; there's some deepish ruts and some stony roads before me, and that's why I were so anxious to stop you just now, sir, that I might tell you all about it, and get a word or two from yourself to give us a bit of encouragement."

"I am truly thankful I can't tell you how thankful," replied the young man. "The Lord has indeed done great things for you, and I shall be only too happy to be helpful to you in any way that I can."

"Thank you, sir, kindly; 'tain't worldly help as I wants from you. I've earned enough for me and Sally to last us as long as we live; and it's almost time as I sold the old van, and settled down somewheres for the rest of my days. But it's just this, sir—I want to do some work for the Lord, who's been and done so much for Sally and me. Now I could, as I said just now, sell the old van and settle down; but then I mightn't be able to do much good, and my old limbs would get stiff for want of my regular exercise, and I should just be snoozing away the rest of my time in a big arm-chair. Now I ain't quite used up, nor Sally neither. So I could keep on the move from place to place, dropping a word for Christ here, and a word there, where I've been used to drop scores of words for the devil; and if you'd put me in the way, I could take a lot of Testaments and other good books with me, and sell 'em instead of the poisonous trash as I used to carry. Now, what do you advise me?"

"You couldn't do better, old friend," replied Horace; "you would be showing then your colours, and doing real work for the Master better far than you could if you settled down."

"Well, I think so too, sir; and you must know that I've begun to do a bit for the Lord already, though in a poor sort of way. I used to sell smuggled goods on the sly, and bad songs and bad books, but I've dropped all that now. You may look my van through, drawers and cupboards and all, every corner of it, and you'll not find a scrap of the bad sort now. Eh! how some of my old customers do stare, and how some on 'em do jeer, when I tells 'em as I've done selling the old things as they delight in. But it don't matter. I've made up my mind, and they're beginning to find that out. They call me an old humbug, and tell me as Sally and I shall end our days in the Union. But I ain't afeard; it ain't the likes of them as can send me there, and I know I'm safe in the Lord's hands."

"That's very true," said Horace; "you'll be taken good care of while you are in the path of duty, and you will have many a noble opportunity of helping on the good cause as you go from place to place. Many will get a word from you which they might not be in the way of hearing otherwise, and the very fact of such a change in the hearts and lives of your wife and yourself must tell on the consciences of many who see what you are now and know what you were in times past.'

"I believe you sir," said the old man. "Now, there's one who's been touched already

—Jim Grimes, who keeps 'The Old Fighting-Cocks' at Bridgepath. He were mightily surprised at first when he seed as I'd given up my old ways; he wouldn't believe as it were the true thing, and he were for chaffing me out of it. But he found out after a bit as I was real. 'Tain't for me to boast—it were the Lord's doings, not mine but when he came to be persuaded as I had taken to the better way in earnest, he couldn't make it out at first; but now he has come to set his feet on the right road, too, I trust, and this has made me think as there's work for the Lord for me to do in a quiet way without giving up the van— in a quiet way, I say, sir, for I don't want to be put in a 'mag.'"

"Put in a 'mug,' old friend!" exclaimed Horace, in amused surprise; "what can you mean? Is it slang for putting you in prison? Why should any one put you in prison for such a work as you are purposing to carry on? If any one tries to get you into trouble, come or send to me; they shan't interfere with you."

"Nay, nay, sir," replied Ruby Grigg, with a

laugh. "Thank you kindly for what you say; but you've not got hold of my meaning. What I'm driving at is this: I don t want people to put me in a 'mag,'—mag's short for 'magazine,' one of them monthly or weekly papers as is full of pictures, and serves as town-crier to all the good deeds as is being done."

"Ah, I understand you now," said Horace, smiling in return; "you want to work quietly for Christ in the shade, and not to be made a public character of."

"That's just it, sir; I wouldn't be put in a 'mag' for all the world. I've knowed many a good man spoilt by being put in a 'mag.' It blows 'em up with pride; and then them as don't get put in the 'mag' is fit to burst with envy and jealousy."

"I believe, my friend," said Horace, "that there may be a great deal of truth in what you say. A good man's usefulness may be injured by his being dragged into public notice; for no sin needs such watchfulness on the part of Christians, especially those at the beginning of their course, as pride. There is too much of this trumpeting in our day, it spoils the simplicity and reality of many a character."

"I've seen it, sir," replied Reuben. "I used to laugh at it formerly, but I grieve over it now. At any rate I'm sure sir, as you won't put me in a 'mag.' I don't want to see myself in a couple of picturs, one with me and my van as they was, and t'other with the likeness of Mister Reuben Gregson in a brand new suit of clothes and a white choker, looking for all the world like a regular parson. 'Twouldn't do me no good. I just want to do a little work in a quiet way—to jog along, telling how the Lord has done great things for me, and just to mix up a few Bibles, and Testaments, and tracts as I'm selling my goods. And I don't want no reward here, and no notice, leastways no public notice. I've had more reward nor I deserve already; and if I make a few kind friends, such as yourself and the colonel maybe, I'd rather do it, Mr. Horace, in a quiet way, and then I shall feel as I'm doing the work for the Lord himself out and out."

"Well, dear old friend," said Horace, "it

shall be as you say, so far as I am concerned, and I can answer for my uncle too. And I feel sure that you are right, I understand now how the change has taken place in James Grimes. Yes, the Lord honours steady consistent example, and I do heartily thank him that he has seen fit to enlist you in the increasing and noble army of 'workers in the shade.'"

XI.

A Surprise.

MR. HORACE JACKSON has completed his twenty first year, and the day is to be marked by a grand gathering in the grounds in front of Park House. The persons invited on the occasion were all the tenants on the estate, the two Misses Stansfield, and Lady Willerly and her daughter. Ruby Grigg also and his wife Sally were present by special invitation.

The colonel had never formally declared that his nephew was to be his heir, though it had been generally understood that such was to be the case. And now the proceedings at Riverton Park were to be of so quiet a character, that people began to question whether after all this celebration of the young man's coming of age might not merely be an ordinary keeping of the majority of one who might not in the end turn out to be the real heir to the property. Such was the conjecture of the public as the preparations were watched and commented upon. "And yet who can tell?" exclaimed ungratified curiosity reproachfully, "for the colonel never does anything like other people." There was, however, one person who was abundantly satisfied, and that was old John Price; but nothing could be got from him, though a host of questioners assailed him as he made his way down to the house, on the morning of the birthday gathering, seated on an old pony as prudent and impenetrable as himself.

It was a glorious day, and, after a hearty noonday meal, all the guests were collected on the lawn in front of the mansion. The colonel, his sister, and their nephew, having dined with the company, now occupied the centre of a group which had gathered on the steps of Park House, consisting of the ladies invited and old John Price. Scarce a sound was heard but the rustling of the leaves of some of the noble trees, as all sat waiting for what was to come next, for certainly something special was expected by all, though they could scarce have told why At last the colonel stood forward, and, raising his hat from his venerable head, just closed his eyes for a moment and murmured a few words to himself and then, his voice trembling at first with emotion, spoke as follows

"My dear friends, I am about to bring strange things to your ears, but I trust not disagreeable ones. And first of all, let me introduce to you, under a new name, Mr Horace Walters, the only son and only child of your late squire, and the present and, I trust for many happy years to come, future proprietor of the Riverton estate."

He paused as the whole company rose to their feet and vociferously cheered the young master. Looks of astonishment and perplexity were then exchanged by many as they resumed their seats, but these soon gave place to most earnest attention to Colonel Dawson, who thus proceeded

"You may some of you be wondering, dear friends, how I can have permitted your dear young squire to have assumed and carried with my sanction a name among you that is not really his own; but I shall soon show you what will, I am sure, be perfectly satisfactory to you all on this point. What I am now going to tell you is not a mere tale to gratify curiosity. I have a sacred duty to perform in telling it; for it was the earnest request that I should do so of one who had a right to claim it of me I mean your late squire, the father of my dear young friend here, whom I shall never cease to call my dear nephew.

"You must know, then, that some twenty-five years have now passed since I retired from the army. I was living at that time in a quiet way in my native county, when a cousin of mine, who used to be my special companion and friend when we were boys, died, and left me, to my considerable surprise, a large property in Australia, in which country he had been living for many years as an extensive sheep farmer. Believing that property has its duties as well as its profits, I resolved to go over and see what my new acquisition was like, and what I had best do with it. I had no thoughts at first of settling in the colony. But I found when I got there a great deal to do and a great deal to undo before things could be set properly in order; and by the time I had got things into shape I had got so used to colonial life, and so well satisfied with its freedom from many of those fetters which society imposes on us in many of her usages in the old mother country, that I made up my mind to settle, for a time at any rate, in my adopted land.

"I had a house of my own in Melbourne, and used to visit my country estate from time to time as I found it necessary. One day, as I was walking along one of the principal streets of the city, when I had been settled in the colony a few years, I noticed a little boy of rather superior appearance, who was neatly but plainly dressed, walking slowly past the shops with a very sad expression on his face and his poor eyes full of tears. I stopped him, and asked what was the matter. He was reluctant at first to tell me; but on my getting his confidence by the sincere interest he saw I took in him, the little fellow told me that his dear old nurse was very ill, and he was afraid she would die before his father came back.

"I went with him at once to his home, which was a very humble one in a side street, and found the poor woman, the child's nurse, quite sensible, yet manifestly near her end. The neighbours had been kind, and had done what they could; but it was too plain that human skill would not avail to restore the old woman to health or prolong her life. But she was quite able to listen to me; and when I had offered a prayer by her bedside, she evidently felt that she could confide her sorrows and troubles to me.

"She told me that her master, the little boy's father, was called William Jackson; that he had come from England a few years before, after the death of his wife, to try his fortune in the colony, having lost his property in England. She herself, having known him from his infancy, and always having lived in his family, came with him to Australia to take care of Horace, his only child, who was then an infant. Her master had found employment in the city, but was anxious to see if he could not meet with success at the gold diggings. He therefore had left her and his little son three months since, and they had only heard from him once. Horace was now six years old, and was going to a day school in the city; and as Mr. Jackson had left a sum of money with her which was not yet exhausted, she was not in want as regarded herself or the child, and was now anxiously looking for the father's return. But it had pleased God to lay her low with sickness; and feeling that her time must be short, she was deeply concerned as to what was to become of her little charge, whom she loved as dearly as if he had been her own.

"I told her not to distress herself on this subject, but to cast this burden on the Lord, and that I would see what could be done. Her poor face lighted up when I said these words; and from the reply which she made, I concluded that she was a pious woman and knew where to lay her cares. So I went home, and after giving the necessary directions for the poor nurse's comfort, I began seriously to consider what was to be done for the poor child; and after putting the matter before the Lord, I resolved to take him into my own house, and treat him as my own till his father should turn up. And so a week later, when the faithful old nurse was buried, I took the little Horace to live with me, and we have never been long separated from that day to this.

"But what of William Jackson, his father? Months rolled on, and no tidings a year, and no tidings. Horace had learned to call me uncle, and I to call him and speak of him as nephew : and though friends and neighbours at first perfectly understood that this was only a loving mode of address, not at all intended to deceive anybody, yet in process of time it became so completely a matter of course with us, that we can hardly either of us believe that this relationship does not really exist between us, and so I shall be 'Uncle Dawson' to him, and he will be 'Nephew Horace' to me till death parts us. Horace was now seven years old, and I felt only too thankful to mark in him the evidences of a real love to that Saviour whom his good old nurse had taught him to know and serve in his childish way. And so the boy was twining himself tight round my heart, and, to tell the honest truth, I began to dread the father's return, and almost to hope he might never come back to claim his child.

"It was one beautiful day in February. You must remember, dear friends, that February is one of our hot months in the southern hemisphere. Horace was at school, and I was sitting by an open window in my private room, which looked on to the garden at the back of my town house. Something came between me and the light. I looked up from my writing. A man stood by the open window, and did not move away as he saw my eyes fixed on him. He wore a broad palm leaf hat, which rather shaded from my view his full features; but I could see a noble countenance, which was rendered strikingly picturesque by the profusion of beard and mustache, which had evidently been long untrimmed. His upper clothing consisted of a faded blouse, fastened round the neck by a black silk handkerchief. He had also coarse duck trousers on, bound round his waist by a leathern belt, and well-made boots on his feet, which were remarkably small for one of his robust make.

"My heart sank within me for a moment or two, for I divined at once who he must be; but, recovering myself, I asked him if he wished to speak with me. 'Yes; he should be glad to do so,' he replied in a sad voice, but with the greatest courtesy of manner.

"He was soon seated opposite to me, and came at once to the point by saying, 'How can I ever discharge my debt of gratitude to you, Colonel Dawson, for your most generous treatment of my poor boy, who might have been lost or ruined but for your kindness?'

"'Pray, don't say anything more on the sub ject, Mr. Jackson,' I replied. 'It has been a happiness to me to have been led to befriend your child; and, indeed, he has become so dear to me, that I know not how to part with him. But, of course, as he is yours, not mine, you are at liberty to take him when you will, or to leave him with me till you can provide a settled home for him.'

"My visitor was greatly moved, and grasped my hand most warmly. 'I know,' he said, 'the best recompense I can make to one who has acted towards me as you have done, is to lay myself under still deeper obligation to you; and I will do so. I may tell you thus much about myself I am not what I seem. I have a great object which I am seeking to accomplish, and I am, I think, on the road to success. I shall be most thankful to leave my boy in your hands, at any rate, for the present, and shall be most happy to charge myself with all his expenses at home and at school.'

"'Nay, Mr. Jackson,' I replied; 'while he remains with me it shall be my privilege to supply him with all that he needs, as I can well afford to do, and I shall be further truly happy to be of personal service to yourself if I can.'

"'I accept your offer with gratitude,' he

replied. 'You *can* help me, I dare say. I want employment as a clerk or book-keeper. Dare you trust me yourself, or dare you recommend me to another? I dare myself affirm that I will not disappoint an employer who may trust me.'

"There was a frankness and sincerity in his manner which completely disarmed me of all suspicion or hesitation; whatever colonial *prudence* might suggest, I *could* not distrust him. So I offered him at once a place in my own office with a moderate stipend. He accepted it without hesitation, and lived in my house as a member of the family; and never did employer have a more intelligent and faithful worker. As for the child, his father never in the least interfered with my management of him, though I brought him up after my own utterly unfashionable, or perhaps more properly speaking, old-fashioned ideas. On the contrary, he warmly approved of my system.

"'I cannot tell you,' he said one day, soon after he had come to live with me, 'how truly grateful I am to see you forming my dear boy's character in the way you are doing. I want him to be the very opposite to what I was myself at his age, and to what the generality of children are now. I was brought up just to please myself and to have my own way to be, in fact, a little incarnation of self-will and selfishness. I was allowed to ask for everything I liked at the table, no restriction being put upon my self indulgence. I went where I liked, and did what I liked, and was never checked except when I was in the way, or had become intolerably troublesome. I was placed under no regular discipline, and was allowed to thrust myself and my opinions forward amongst my seniors and those who were my superiors in everything but worldly position; and as I grew older, and became inconveniently self asserting, I was alternately snubbed and humoured according to the whim or temper of those who claimed authority over me. And what was the result? Alas! early reckless extravagance followed by ruin, and a character which might have been moulded into something noble, now for a long time shapeless and distorted. And my boy—well, I am only too thankful that he has fallen into your hands out of his unworthy father's.' He spoke these words with deep emotion.

"'I am truly glad, Mr. Jackson,' I said, 'that you are able to look at things in this better and clearer light. I quite agree with you about the present bringing up of children. For a few years they are treated as little idols by parents, who are too selfish to give themselves the pain and trouble of correcting and disciplining them, and this, too, even in cases where the parents themselves are true Christians; and then, when they begin to get unbearable, and have passed out of the winning ways of early childhood, they are too often thrown back upon themselves, and made to suffer the penalty of neglect of discipline and training, which ought properly to be inflicted on the parents, who have not done their duty towards them.'

"'It is so. I have seen it; I have felt it, Colonel Dawson,' he replied warmly; 'and so I just leave Horace's education entirely in your hands.'

"And thus it was that I brought up my dear nephew, as I still continued to call him, in my own way—that is to say, to eat what was given him, to do what was told him, to go where I allowed him, and to have as much liberty as I thought good for him; to listen when his elders were speaking, to be diligent in his lessons, early in his hours of rising and going to bed, and regular in all his habits. And he will tell you himself, I don't doubt, as he has told me over and over again, that, so far from feeling this discipline and these wholesome restraints a bondage, he was as happy as the day was long under them. And I am sure of this, dear friends, that the little, stuck-up, pampered, self willed, selfish children which abound in our day, who are supposed to rejoice in having their own way, are really slaves to themselves, as well as a burden to their friends, and are strangers to that vigorous enjoyment which is the privilege of a childhood passed under judicious and even discipline.

"Well, so it was with Horace; and so his father rejoiced to find it. And what made me rejoice still more was the happy conviction that a deeper work still was beginning to manifest itself in the heart and life of the dear boy. Yes, you may think it strange, dear friends that I am entering into all these particulars on an occasion so public as the present, and with your young squire by my side; but I have a reason for it, as you will see by-and by. and I am doing it with the full consent and approval of my dear nephew himself. Let me, then, proceed with my story.

"When Horace was sixteen years of age he expressed to me his earnest desire to engage in some special work for the spread of the gospel. which he had learned himself to prize above all earthly things. His father at this time was not residing with me in the town, but held the post of manager of my country estate and sheep farm, which flourished admirably under his most vigorous and faithful superintendence; for he was a born ruler of others, and a man of such decision of character that everything he laid his hands to fell, as it were, into order under his unflagging and indomitable energy.

I knew that I had 'the right man in the right place,' and was satisfied. However, when his son expressed this his heart's desire to me, we rode up together to my country house and laid the matter before Mr. Jackson.

"He seemed at first confused and embarrassed when I mentioned the subject to him, and asked me to wait for his views upon it till the following day. So we spent the night at the farm; and the next day the father and myself walked towards the neighbouring hills, and then he told me, what you may be sure I was deeply thankful to hear, that what he was pleased to call the consistent Christianity which he had witnessed in our household had been blessed to himself, and that he trusted that he was now endeavouring to live as a true follower of his Saviour.

"'You will approve, then,' I said, 'of Horace's wish to be trained for direct gospel work.'

"'Yes and no,' he replied. 'By *no*,' he added, 'I mean that I do not wish him to enter the ministry. I have reasons of my own for this which just now I would rather keep to myself;

but one day, and it may be before very long, I should like you to know them.'

"'And what would you wish, then, Horace to do?' I asked.

"'I will talk the matter over with him,' he said. And he did so that day; and the result was that the young man proposed, with his father's full approbation, to pass through a course of training in medicine and surgery with a view to his becoming qualified for the post of medical missionary. So, on our return to Melbourne, the necessary steps were taken; and two years ago my nephew left us for a short experimental trip to one of the islands of the Pacific Ocean, under the guidance of an excellent and experienced missionary.

"And now I am coming to a very sad and wonderful part of my story; but as I have talked long enough now to weary myself if not to weary you, I will ask you to amuse yourselves for a while among the grounds and in the park till tea-time, and after tea I shall be happy to conclude my story, the most important part of which is yet to come."

XII.

Cloud and Sunshine.

THERE was clearly much anxiety on the part of the guests to hear the conclusion of Colonel Dawson's narrative. So the bountiful tea which had been provided was speedily despatched, and every eye fixed intently on the speaker when he resumed his address, after the tables had been withdrawn and the hearers settled in their old places.

"You will remember," began the colonel, "that I had sorrowful things to tell you in continuing my story; and sorrowful indeed they are, though not without a mixture of brightness. Horace had been gone from the colony, on what I might call his missionary trial trip, about a month, when I was one day sitting alone under the veranda of my country house, thinking over many things, and specially pondering the wonderful way in which I had gained two so dear to me as Horace and his father. Then my thoughts and heart went across the sea to my dear nephew, when I was suddenly aroused from my day-dream by seeing just before me a stranger, who must have come up very silently, for I was quite unaware of his approach till I looked up and saw him gazing very keenly and not very pleasantly at me. It was now evening, and twilight, of which there is very little in those parts, would speedily be followed by darkness. The newcomer was dressed in bush fashion, and carried a rifle, and I could see the stocks of a brace of pistols peeping out from his blouse. The man's features and appearance altogether were most forbidding; and though a military man myself, I felt anything but comfortable with these ferocious eyes staring full upon me. However, in the bush open house is more or less a rule, and rough looking fellows often turn up and request a night's lodging and food, which we do not think of refusing them. Besides which, the wild-looking outside not unfrequently covers an honest heart beneath. So, while I did not at all like the looks of my visitor, I asked him what he wanted, and if he would sit down and take some refreshment. He replied, in a voice as rough as his appearance, that he was looking after some horses which had strayed as he was bringing them overland, and that he should be glad of a mouthful of bread and cheese and a drink. The refreshment was brought him by one of my men, whom he eyed all over; while all the time he was eating, those same fierce and restless eyes were taking in everything about the place, till he rose to go, with a muttered word or two which hardly sounded like thanks.

"No sooner was he out of sight than Horace's father joined me in the veranda. His voice was agitated as he asked,

"'Do you know that man?'

"'Not that I am aware of,' I replied; 'indeed I may say, certainly not; for once seen, such a man is not easily forgotten. A more villanous face I never beheld.'

"'You may well say so,' said my friend. 'I know that man too well, he nearly succeeded in taking my life at the diggings, he is somewhat older looking, of course, but there is no mistaking him. He was an escaped convict when I knew him, and belonged to the most dangerous set in the place where 'I was working. I don't at all like his lurking about here. You may depend upon it, his presence bodes no good.'

"'I can well believe that,' I said; 'so we must take proper precautions, and see that the men are on the look-out.'

"'Yes,' he replied, 'I will see to that; and it will be as well to send a messenger to-night over to Melbourne to give the police a hint, as I fancy they would not be sorry to come across this fellow, as his doings are no doubt pretty well known to them.'

"Nothing more occurred that night to disturb us; but the following day four horsemen might be seen riding up towards the house at a dashing gallop, just about noon. I was prepared, however, for their coming and had caused all the men about the place to take refuge in my own house, which I had made provision for barricading it necessary. I had only three or four men on the place at that time, and their wives and children. These last I brought into an inner room when I saw the horsemen in the distance. Though a soldier by profession, I was exceedingly reluctant to shed blood, and had resolved on the present occasion not to do so if it could possibly be avoided.

"The strangers were soon at the veranda, evidently resolved to take us by storm. Foremost among them was my visitor of the day before. He sprang down from his horse in the most reckless manner, and began thundering at the door with the butt end of his rifle. My house had not been built with the view of its sustaining a siege at any time, but was constructed of rather light materials, so that the door began to groan and creak under the assaults of the bushranger, whose every movement I could see through a small opening in the shutters.

"'What do you want here friend?' I asked.

"'Open the door,' was the only reply.

"'Tell me what you want,' I said again.

"'Open the door,' was all that was returned in answer; and then came a thundering blow, which fairly crushed in one of the panels.

"'Shall I fire?' asked Mr. Jackson, in a hoarse whisper.

"'No, no! not yet, not yet,' I cried.

"Then came a united rush of three of the men, and the door came crashing into the outer room. The foremost villain then sprang at me, and we wrestled together, after I had knocked up his revolver. In a few minutes I had hurled him back from me, and he fell to the ground and was seized by one of my men. Gasping for breath, I paused and looked about me. A pistol was presented at me by another bushranger, but before it could be fired Horace's poor father had thrown himself in front of me; he received the bullet in his own breast, and fell to the ground grievously wounded. But now help was at hand, alas that it did not come sooner! A strong body of mounted police came up, and having secured all the robbers, carried them off in triumph.

"But what was to be done with my dear wounded friend, who had saved my life by perilling his own? I knew enough of surgical matters to ascertain by inspection that the injury, though severe, was not likely to be mortal. So, having bandaged up the wound with the best appliances I had at hand, I drove my friend as rapidly as he could bear it to my town house, where he was at once placed under the care of the best medical skill in the city. And for some time I had every hope that he would recover, and earnestly did I pray that it might be so, if it were the Lord's will. But it was not so to be. A constitution once strong, but impaired in early youth, and much tried when he was at the diggings, had not sufficient vigour remaining to enable my poor friend to regain health and strength. But he did not pass away rapidly, nor did he lose any of his power of mind in his last days. And then it was, on his dying bed, that he opened his whole heart to me, and told me what I am about to tell you, and, as nearly as I can remember, in these words:

"'My name is really Horace Walters, and I am the owner of an estate called Riverton Park in my dear native country. But I ruined myself by my mad love for gambling, and when my poor wife died, and left me with Horace a baby, and my estate was become sadly encumbered, I resolved at once that I would leave my native land, go over to Australia, live a life of hard work and self-denial, and not come back again until, by the accumulated rents and by what I could earn, I could make my property absolutely and honestly my own, and leave it unencumbered to my dear child. You have seen enough of me to know that I have some strength of will in my character; and so, when I had made this resolution, I began immediately to carry it out. Taking with me our old nurse, whom I bound to secrecy, I came over to this colony, got employment, and then went to the diggings.

There, by diligence, perseverance, and self denial, I managed to accumulate a large sum, which is safely deposited in the bank. I had some thoughts of going back at once to England; but on learning what had happened to Horace, and about your noble and loving care of him, I resolved to wait a while, and to get employment in your neighbourhood at any rate, for a time. And that resolution I have never repented of; indeed, I have felt *my* dear Horace's ay, I will say *our* dear Horace's position in your house such a privileged one, that I have gladly delayed taking any further steps homeward, wishing to see him all that we both could desire him to be before I let him know his real name and position. You can easily understand why I changed my name to Jackson. I felt that I had brought shame and dishonour on my own name in my native land and I resolved that in this distant country I would change it for another, and not take it back again till I could do so with honour and credit to myself and my child.'

" And then, dear friends, he told me how he

blessed God for bringing himself to the knowledge of his truth, and me for having been the instrument an unworthy one indeed I was of leading him to that knowledge. Of course, I told him what a privilege I felt it to have been permitted to guide him to his Saviour; and I added that I would gladly do anything I could to show my gratitude to him for having sacrificed himself to save my life.

"'You have done more than enough already,' was his reply; 'and yet I will take you at your word. Horace knows nothing yet of his real name and prospects; I had made up my mind lately that I would wait till he came of age to tell him. And now I would ask you, dear friend, to take Horace with you to England and see him settled in his property when I am gone, which will be, I know, before very long. I have ample means in the bank here to meet all expenses, and will give you full power to act for me. You will understand now why I did not wish Horace to be a minister. I think godly laymen are as much needed as godly clergymen; and, as he in God's providence inherits an important property, I have a strong impression that he will be more free to do his duty to his tenantry and his estate as a Christian country squire, than he would be if he had taken upon himself the charge of a special sphere or parish at home or abroad. And my earnest wish and prayer is that he may soon, by his conduct as a Christian landlord, blot out altogether the memory of his unworthy father.'

"I stopped him here and told him that he was nobly redeeming the past, so far as it was possible for man to do so, and that I would gladly carry out what he desired. This seemed to make him quite happy; and his one great wish now was to see his son once more, and this was granted to him. Horace returned to comfort him in his dying hours, and to receive his blessing, with his expressed wish that he should accompany me to England, whither I was going on his account to settle some matters of business for him. He said nothing further to his son, having already expressed his wish to me that I should first set the Riverton estate in thorough order, according to my own views of what was right with one special injunction, that I should do everything that might be in my power to recompense John Price and his family for the loss they had suffered on his account.

"So, after my poor friend's departure to his better inheritance, we have come over here to carry out his wishes and instructions; and you have seen, and can now see, the results. My dear nephew has been kept in ignorance of his real name and prospects till yesterday, when I laid the whole matter before him; and it is by his father's earnest dying request that I have given you this full and minute history. To-day Horace Walters is of full age, and to-day I surrender up all to him.

"I would just add a word or two more. I have gone so fully into my story, not only because Mr. Walters urged me to do so, but still more for two special reasons: first, because I know that rumour and fancy would be sure to put their heads together and circulate all sorts of foolish stories about your late squire, and about his dear son, your present squire, and some of these stories probably to the discredit of one or both. Now I have given you the true account of all, so that you can safely put down all slanderers' gossip and tittle-tattle on the subject. And further, I have gone thus particularly into my story, because it will show you what rare jewels there were in your late squire's character, and how brightly those shone out when the black crust of evil habits had fallen away from them. And, lastly, I have wished to show you how graciously God has been ordering things for the good of you all, and has brought blessings and peace out of a strange tangle of circumstances which he has unravelled for your happiness.

"And now, dear friends having accomplished the work for which I came back to the old country, I am returning to the land of my adoption for a time. I think it will be only for a time; for my dear nephew here has got such a hold upon my heart, that I think I shall have to come back and settle near him, if I am spared. However, I have the satisfaction of knowing that I am leaving behind me two earnest, like minded servants of the great Master to preside over the good work at Riverton and Bridgepath. I shall not leave the country till I have seen them made one; and then I shall feel assured that in Horace Walters and her who will, I trust, soon become his wife, I shall leave you those who, having long been working for God separately in the shade, will work together as devotedly, hand in hand, and heart in heart, in the light.'

THE END.

www.ingramcontent.com/pod-product-compliance
Lightning Source LLC
Chambersburg PA
CBHW031448160426
43195CB00010BB/896